money

money

A USER'S GUIDE

LAURA WHATELEY

4th Estate • London

4th Estate
An imprint of HarperCollins*Publishers*
1 London Bridge Street
London SE1 9GF

www.4thEstate.co.uk

First published in Great Britain in 2018 by 4th Estate

1

A catalogue record for this book is available from the British Library

ISBN 978-0-00-830831-5

The information in this book is for general guidance only and is not
legal advice. If you need more details on your rights or legal advice about
what action to take, please see an advisor or solicitor. Please note that neither
HarperCollins nor the Author offer investmant advice. All financial
investments carry risk. You should therefore seek independant
financial advice before making any investment.

Printed and bound by CPI Group (UK) Ltd, Croydon, CR0 4YY

MIX
Paper from
responsible sources
FSC™ C007454

This book is produced from independently certified FSC paper
to ensure responsible forest management.

For more information visit: www.harpercollins.co.uk/green

To Mum and Dad

CONTENTS

money

INTRODUCTION

This is a little guide that I could have really done with ten years ago, when I was twenty-three, and fresh off a First Great Western into London, one of the world's most expensive cities, ready to start my first full-time job as the global economy crashed. Here I address the things I wish I had known about money earlier (the younger you start saving the more time your money has to grow) but was too embarrassed to ask. I assumed everybody else already had it nailed. Turns out that most did not, and still don't, whatever their seeming competency at being an adult.

My aim is to make sense to those of you who write yourselves off as bad with money, the way I once did and often still do, as you stare down the barrel of your overdraft. It does not have to always be this way. Anyway, what does being bad with money even mean? Failing to check your bank balance regularly and not putting enough in a pension? Or putting so much in your pension that you haven't had a holiday since 2005? Who is to judge?

Here is a secret: everyone is 'bad' with their money sometimes, some people are just better at styling it out and not letting on, some are rich enough that they can keep it well hidden. We are psychologically programmed to make poor financial decisions. There's a whole Nobel-prize-winning area of academia, known as behavioural economics, to describe how. And because no one likes talking about money, and no two people agree on what it is for, whether it is better to spend it or to save it (clue, there is no right answer), the myth that others know what they are doing is rarely exposed.

•

So read on if you have ever wanted to know, what actually is an ISA? What tax do I pay and why? How much should I be saving towards retirement? Should I be investing any money, and if so, how? Should I pay off my student loan? How do mortgages work? What are the best budgeting apps? How do I split money with my other half fairly, and can I ever afford to buy a home, bring up a child, or be the kind of person at ease in small-plate restaurants?

What stupid mistakes am I making with my money, and how can I stop it making me feel so crap about myself?

Get through this in an afternoon, and you should know a lot more than you did this morning. I can guarantee that if you follow at least a couple of tips in this book you will have already reimbursed the cover price.

But first, a bit about me, us feckless 'millennials', and where we are at.

Please note that I use the term 'millennial' reluctantly. It is a word that has come to make me itchy, a crude catch-all for the 14 million or so very different people born between the early 1980s and the year 2000, some of whom are now parents of teenagers, your boss, your lawyer, your surgeon, or your favourite novelist.

In September 2008 I went for an interview for a role as editorial assistant on the Money section at *The Times*, the optimistic move of a young graduate not yet grown into the full self-doubt phase. The night before, I'd been up late Wikipeding 'what is a mortgage?'

The timing of this interview, the beginning of my career so far, was significant, though I didn't see how at the time. Two weeks earlier the world's fourth-largest investment bank, Lehman Brothers, had collapsed. The headline on the front page of *The Times* on the day of my interview was alarming: 'the eye of the storm', with a photograph of black clouds gathering over the White House. The introduction read:

> The financial system lurched closer to a catastrophic breakdown last night after the US Congress dramatically rejected a bailout plan designed to restore confidence to paralysed banks. Wall Street suffered one of its worst days in history.

> In 24 hours five banks across the West, including Britain's Bradford & Bingley, had to be rescued to avoid insolvency . . . the Dow Jones industrial average of shares dived almost 800 points, losing 7 per cent of its value. It was the worst one-day points fall and the worst percentage fall since Black Monday in 1987.

I had little understanding of what all this meant ('Dow Jones industrial average', eh?). Nor many of the increasingly panicked headlines that followed over the next few weeks: 'World takes fright' . . . 'The scramble to sell: £2.7 trillion wiped off the global value of shares' . . . 'Banks nationalized' . . . 'Slump pushes jobless towards 2 million'.

I would learn, as I explained hopefully to my new editors. They, unbelievably, took me on. A money journalist is one of those things, like Tupperware and condoms, that you need more of in a recession.

Exactly a decade later, still writing for *The Times* about consumer affairs, now helping readers with their financial woes and blunders as the consumer champion known as 'Troubleshooter', I see how much those few weeks changed the world, not least for those of us who received our first pay cheques in the period since the financial crisis took hold.

Lots has improved, as I'll explain through this book. Banks are desperate to win back our trust, and technology has created countless new opportunities to make it easier to manage money well. But there has been a lasting difficult legacy, especially for those, such as my sister, who are a few years younger than me. Most under-thirties, however diligent, will never be able to buy a decent-sized home in a great part of an exciting British city on their salary alone, especially not while their incomes are reduced by student loans for decades and they are simultaneously trying to save enough into a pension to afford their heating bills when they reach ninety.

Jobs are insecure, wages static. Many, whatever their age, now work longer hours in smaller teams of staff, doing more for relatively less money than their seniors ever did at the same age. The spectre lingers of another recession and a further round of redundancies.

This is coupled with navigating the money-related dilemmas that come as part and parcel of growing up, whatever generation you were born into: how to become financially independent from your parents, how to work out money with your friends without being consumed by status anxiety, how to provide both for yourself and for your family, how to earn more and spend less without missing out on the things that make you happy and life worth living.

I also believe our ability to feel good about money is diminished by the fact that the financial services world loves to obfuscate. A lot of companies make their profit by exploiting our ignorance of how their products really work, maybe cynically, or maybe just because they too overestimate how financially competent their clients really are.

There is a move towards greater transparency, but there is a long way to go. Meanwhile the paralysing choice of financial products out there grows into a dizzying, offputting blur of numbers, percentages and jargon. There are, as I detail in my chapter on household bills, now about half a million subtly different mobile and broadband deals available to 'choose' from. Going to the pub is better by far than boring yourself to tears trawling moneysupermarket.com, and everyone who advertises on the site knows it.

The following chapters are a compilation of advice and tips I have picked up about personal finance since the credit crunch and since my student days, inspired by making my own myriad money mistakes while observing and writing about the traps that *Times* readers have fallen into.

IMPORTANT DISCLAIMER: I am very much not a financial adviser. The only post-school exams I passed involved words (apart from a first-year university statistics and maths resit that continues to give me stress dreams). I'm just a journalist. None of this book constitutes official, legally watertight, financial advice. What it offers are observations and suggestions formed by speaking to real qualified experts, researchers and proper financial advisers about how to avoid common errors.

Even so, I hope this information will help equip you with enough money basics to feel more confident about your own situation and whether or not you can improve it. I hope it will offer a glimpse into how to make better, more informed, more ethical choices, and how to avoid being mugged off by your bank and your mobile-phone network, which will save you far more money than cutting back on a few brunches ever can.

Good luck! If I can do it, so can you. Seriously.

. . . .

Who this book is for, and how to read it

To state the obvious, the best advice on how to manage your money varies depending on how much of it you have and what stage of life you are at. This presents a dilemma when writing a shortish book. I had to make some decisions about who to address, what to include and what to leave out. I have chosen to focus on advice that I think is most practical for people under the age of forty, who have probably borrowed money to study, and who are earning enough to pay tax and rent a home privately, possibly working out whether or not they can afford to buy their first place.

Most of the advice applies to the whole of the UK, but in some cases laws and processes – such as how to buy a house – differ slightly in Scotland, Northern Ireland and Wales. If you don't live in England and are in doubt, please check.

There are also things I mention that change year by year – tax allowances, for example, a company's financial products, or government policy – which may mean that some of what I say here falls out of date. I have written with figures, laws and product recommendations true of autumn 2018.

I write appreciating with respect that there are millions of people in the UK who have to manage on minimum wages, and rely on benefits and food banks. There are millions of Brits who could not fathom having enough cash to invest in the stock market, or contemplate buying their own home in an area of their choosing. I have also carried out research for this book by chatting to some baby boomers and some pensioners who, just like those under forty, said they could really do with tips on how to save more and spend less. So while this book may appeal most to a younger, wealthier-than-average demographic, I hope people of all ages and financial means may find something that helps them in here, whether it is to understand how to get a better deal on your energy, get help to cope with unmanageable debt, decide whether or not you should make a will, or pick the most suitable bank account.

The book has three parts. You can read it in order, or pick out any chapter – they each stand alone – to get some advice on a particular topic that is relevant or concerning to you, such as how to understand your pension.

In **PART ONE** I go through the areas of personal finance that I think are most relevant to the under-forties, starting with housing and borrowing, through to how to budget, where to put aside savings for your short- and long-term future, and how to understand and reduce both your household bills and the amount of tax you are paying.

In **PART TWO** I look at how money makes us feel about ourselves and our relationships, offer some advice gathered from counsellors about how to deal with our emotions around money, as well as some practical tips on how to split it while cohabiting. I detail how to manage money if you feel that it is making you unhappy, or exacerbating an existing mental-health condition.

If you read most of the chapters in sequence you should have enough of a grasp of your finances by the end of Part Two to decide whether you want to do something better with them, not just to make yourself richer, but with consideration for wider society.

PART THREE looks at the growing, and important, shift towards arranging our personal finances ethically, from checking the source of the energy you use, to where to invest your pension, in a way that is mindful of its impact on the environment and other people. Being good with your money is not just about making more of it.

PART ONE

1
The housing crisis and how to rent well

Where better to start than with the generation-defining money issue for anyone under forty: where the hell can we afford to live? If arctic rolls and the threat of nuclear war shaped those that came of age in the Seventies, so the Noughties kids have had the Spice Girls, MSN Messenger and a housing crisis.

In November 2017 the estate agent Strutt & Parker (which sells what I would consider to be largely unaffordable properties: a £525,000 cottage in a hamlet outside Totnes, Devon; a £25 million house in Notting Hill, London) issued a report that blew up on Twitter about how first-time buyer couples should be able to save the average £33,000 needed for a UK house deposit, or the insane £64,000 needed for a London house deposit, within just five years by cutting down on six 'luxuries'.

Some of the numbers: give up one night out a week and save £6,000 annually (that assumes you spend £115 a week on one night out) and £2,640 a year on takeaways (£50 a week!). Make rather than buy sandwiches for another £2,576 (£49.50 a week, but you should still eat lunch over the next five years, and bread is not normally free) and eliminate £832 a year on lottery tickets (£16 a week. Anyone?).

Even after finding that, having given up excessive expenditure that you are unlikely to be making, you are still short if buying in London, here comes the kicker:

'Those lucky enough to have family that can help will receive an [additional] average of £29,400 towards their goal.'

Whichever way you want to spin it, however much money you think us under-thirty-fives are wasting on Deliveroo, the statistics are tough to argue away. Average house prices have far outstripped average earnings across the UK, which makes it way more expensive than it used to be to buy a house in every part of the country.

In the South East, where, still, many of the most prestigious and lucrative graduate jobs are to be found, it is particularly bad, with London house prices 15.7 times higher than average incomes for people between the ages of twenty-five and thirty-four, according to a report from February 2018 by the think tank the Institute for Fiscal Studies (IFS). Across Great Britain as a whole nearly 40 per cent of twenty-five to thirty-five year olds face a house price to income ratio of at least 10.

A separate report by the Office of National Statistics (ONS) found that in 2017 the price of a home in London was 13 times the wages of full-time workers aged twenty-two to twenty-nine, in 1999 it was 3.9 times the then average salaries. Even in the North East they are 5.5 times, up from 2.46 in 1999.

Bear in mind, as outlined in chapter 2, my guide to whether or not you can afford to buy. You are unlikely to be able to borrow more than four or five times your salary in a mortgage.

Whenever such statistics appear in the press there follows the same reductive, crabby response: 'Whilst house ownership has collapsed the stag/hen do market in Marbella or Prague has soared,' one man wrote on thetimes.co.uk. But there was another comment on the coverage of the IFS report that sums it up for me, from someone who says she bought a modest semi in the South East in the 1970s.

> It cost £11,500 and I saved a £2,000 deposit (lived with parents), and got a £10,000 mortgage (three times my salary).

> I earned around the national average wage, and the house was around four times the national

average wage. I drove an Austin 1100 which cost £100 and expired a year later. A bit of a struggle, but not too bad.

Similar houses in the same estate are now selling for 15 times the average wage. The cheapest flat in my area is seven to eight times the average wage. That's the problem. For sure iPhones, £3 lattes, and holidays don't help, but they are not the fundamental issue.

FYI, if you went on fifty-two lavish £500 stag or hen dos (sympathies), one every weekend for a whole year, you would have spent £26,000. A typical 20 per cent house deposit in London is now more than £80,000, according to Nationwide Building Society.

With that in mind it makes sense to start any advice on housing with some tips on how to rent well. A third of those born between 1981 and 2000 will be tenants for the rest of their lives, according to the think tank the Resolution Foundation.

I will then move on in chapter 2 to help you work out whether or not you can afford to buy a home, and if you can, how to sort out your credit score, and get yourself the best mortgage possible.

The majority of perma-tenants will be so because they cannot raise a housing deposit big enough to buy close to where they work. I think it is worth stressing, though, that for some people renting is not a result of being unable to buy, but a positive lifestyle decision and a better way of spending, or saving, their salary.

The rental market is riddled with problems, shyster letting agents and landlords promoting property that is not fit for human habitation. Moving constantly between rental properties can be horrendous, as is not knowing when you are going to be booted out or when your rent is going to be raised. Such uncertainty is damaging to mental and physical health, children's schooling, general morale, your confused cat and your wilting pot plants. All the same, for some tenants spending income on rent offers a better, more flexible, sociable way of existing than tying themselves to a hefty mortgage and a resulting nine-to-five grind for the rest of their days. Maybe you don't want to carry the responsibility of fixing a leaking roof.

So: you are renting, out of necessity or out of choice. How do you make the best of it?

How to rent a place and lessen the chances of getting ripped off

Should you rent from a letting agent, or a landlord?

When renting privately you will either do so direct from a landlord or through a letting agency. There are pros and cons of each. Going direct to a landlord helps keep fees down, and you may not have to submit to a credit check. Rents can be cheaper because landlords are not paying someone else to find and check tenants for them. I am also convinced that letting agents play a large part in encouraging landlords to raise rents. Cut out the middleman and you may charm your landlord into wanting to hang on to you without charging more. Reliable tenants are assets.

Sites such as Open Rent, No Agent and Homerenter match up tenants and landlords direct, though you may have to pay some low fees if a landlord wants to see a reference.

Going through a letting agent might help if you need repairs doing, when the agent can negotiate with your landlord on your behalf. You also have more consumer protection by signing up to rent through a letting agency. **Agents must be part of a redress scheme, such as the Property Ombudsman (TPO), The Property Redress Scheme, and Ombudsman Services: Property. You can turn to these organizations for help with any disputes you may have with your landlord or agent. Check an agent's membership before you commit.**

The massive downside to letting agents is fees. For years letting agents have been making an absolute packet out of charging rip-off fees for it's hardly clear what – 'admin', 'renewal', 'referencing'. The housing charity Shelter says the average letting-agent fees are £200, but has seen cases where tenants are charged £700 before they have paid any deposit. The good news is that the government is to outlaw fees for granting or renewing a tenancy in England and Wales, so by 2019 they should no longer exist (they are already banned in Scotland). Agents will only be able to charge for the rent, a refundable holding deposit and security deposit, and any 'default fees', which are penalties in the event that a tenant breaches a clause in their tenancy agreement.

There is concern, however, that agents might exploit this loophole to charge really unreasonable default fees for silly breaches. Shelter has seen people fined for leaving a jar of peanut butter in the cupboard, or failing to remove dust from skirting boards (£3 per skirting board), or totally over-the-top fees for replacing something missing from the inventory, like £100 for a new loo seat when you can buy one for £12.50 in the shops. If you are in this situation, challenge it.

What fees you have to pay up front, and questions to ask before you part with them

When you have found a property you want to rent you will generally need to go through a credit-check process (if you are worried about your credit history see chapter 2 on how to improve it), which is where you are rated on how likely you are to pay your rent on time. You may also need to show bank statements and provide references, such as your old landlord or employer, or failing that, to offer a guarantor, such as a parent, who will agree to cover your rent if you cannot meet it. You then have to cough up a lot of money for a deposit.

Some agents or landlords require a holding deposit, which is a sum of rent paid to secure the property you want while the letting agent checks your references. When the new law comes into force in 2019 a holding deposit can be no more than a week's rent. Do not pay until you are sure you want the property, because you may not be able to get this deposit back if you don't. Usually it will be taken off your tenancy deposit. Get the holding-deposit details in writing, including what will happen to it if your landlord changes their mind and you can't move in.

You usually also have to pay your first month's rent in advance. You then need to add on the tenancy deposit. From 2019 tenancy deposits will be capped at a maximum of six weeks' rent.

Always get receipts whenever you pay anything, in case there are any issues further down the line. Before you pay or sign, see if you can negotiate on any fees or the cost of the rent. These things are not fixed and agents or landlords may be trying it on.

You also need to ask a few questions: how and when you will be paying rent, and whether the rent includes any bills; how long you can rent for – the length of your tenancy – and whether you are entitled to end it early. Are there any rules on what you can and can't do in the flat – for example, have parties, keep a dog, smoke?

Ask to see the property's Energy Performance Certificate (EPC). Legally a property you rent must have an energy-efficiency rating of at least E, unless it is exempt, in which case there is a register for exempt properties on gov.uk. If the property is an F or G your landlord is breaking the law and can be fined.

If you are moving into a shared house with several flatmates your home should be licensed with the local council as a house in multiple occupation (HMO) to make sure it is safe and not at risk of overcrowding. This is worth checking.

Also, it may sound obvious, but do actually view the property you want to rent in situ, rather than just online, before parting with any cash. There are lots of online rental scams out there, particularly targeting students, where you pay upfront fees to secure properties that either do not actually exist or have already been rented out, sometimes multiple times.

Need to know: what are tenancies?

Most private renters will sign an assured shorthold tenancy. Have a good read of the tenancy agreement before you sign it, which lays out what responsibilities your landlord has and how to end or renew your tenancy. Make sure you are given a written tenancy agreement, one in five millennial renters told consumer group Which? that they did not get one when moving. Most shorthold tenancies last six or twelve months, and you have to pay the agreed rent for this whole period. After this fixed period you can agree a new contract, or allow the tenancy to continue. If you want to leave at the end of the fixed term you probably need to give written notice in advance; your agreement should tell you how much notice you need to give. A landlord can end your tenancy without reason – outside of the fixed period – but needs to give you at least two months' written notice, and provided that your leaving date falls at least six months after your original tenancy began.

If you are living with other people you may sign a joint tenancy agreement. This means that you are all responsible for rent, and for sticking to the terms of your agreement. If your flatmate moves out and refuses to pay rent, you will be lumbered with it instead, so pick your roomies carefully.

How your deposit is protected

Landlords have to keep your deposit safe by putting it into a deposit-protection scheme within thirty days of you paying it, or will ask a letting agent to protect your deposit for them. The deposit has to be in a government scheme, and your landlord needs to tell you which one. There are three: Deposit Protection Service (DPS), Tenancy Deposit Scheme (TDS) and My Deposits. They are also allowed to use an insurance scheme to protect it, instead.

You may be given a 'repayment ID' from the scheme. Keep it safe: you need it to get your deposit back at the end of your tenancy.

How do I get my deposit back?

Landlords can only deduct money from your deposit for damage, cleaning costs if you have left the place in a worse state than when you moved in, and any missing items. Their right to do this needs to be detailed in your tenancy agreement. They cannot deduct money for normal wear and tear – for example, scuffs on the walls or faded carpets. Damage needs to be things like a massive iron burn in the middle of the floor.

Check your agreement to see whether you are supposed to have the property professionally cleaned before you move out.

You will agree an inventory when you first move in: a document detailing what is in the property and its condition. Take lots of photos, inside and out, to make a record of any existing issues. You might also want to take photos of the property to show what it is like as you move out, and do a check-out inventory, getting your landlord to sign it, as your back-up if there is any dispute.

You have to contact your landlord or letting agent to request your deposit back. Best do it by email or in writing, so that you have evidence of the date. You should get it back within ten days. If they refuse, or take longer, or if you don't agree with any deductions they make, you can contact the deposit-protection scheme where your money is kept and go through their free dispute-resolution process. If your landlord has made any deductions they should write to you to explain how much and why.

Shelter has a useful template letter on its site to help you challenge any deductions that you think are unfair. As a last resort you could go to the small claims court if you still cannot get back your deposit.

How you can avoid paying an upfront deposit

If you can't afford to pay a large deposit up front there are some new products available to help you get around it. Companies like the Zero Deposit Scheme (ZDS) and Reposit offer what is basically an insurance policy for the landlord instead. With both you pay the equivalent of one week's rent (rather than the normal six required for most security deposits); with ZDS you also pay a £26 annual admin fee for each additional year you are in the same property, and it guarantees to cover your landlord for the same sum as a traditional security deposit.

You will end up paying more with these schemes, however, because most tenants do get their full security deposit back at the end of a tenancy, whereas the money you are paying to the schemes is non-refundable. You are also still liable to pay your landlord directly for any damage that might otherwise have come out of the security deposit. Such schemes are only to be used if you are desperate to move into a rental but really not able to scrape together the cash up front.

Increasingly there are housing developers creating build-to-rent schemes that do not require a security deposit. Two of my friends live in one of the first, by Get Living London, in the old athletes' village in the Olympic Park, London. They also have a longer-term tenancy, of a guaranteed minimum three years. Look out for similar developments.

Who is responsible for repairs in my rental?

Your landlord is legally responsible for keeping your property in decent shape and carrying out timely repairs to its structure – things like pipes and wiring, and heating and hot water – as well as clearing anything that will damage your health, such as mice or mould. You need to do a few basics yourself – change lightbulbs or replace smoke-alarm batteries.

If you are without heating or hot water your landlord should sort it out very quickly. Under section 11 of the Landlord and Tenant Act 1985 a landlord has to supply adequate space, heating and water. The minimum heating standard is at least 18°C in sleeping rooms, and 21°C in living rooms, when the temperature outside is as cold as minus 1°C, and it should be available at all times, according to The Tenants' Voice, which has template letters you can send to your landlord to get them to recognize their responsibilities if they refuse to do so. Always send requests for repairs on email so that you have a record.

Failing that, you can contact the environmental health department at your local council, which can force your landlord to sort the issue, or even authorize repairs and send your landlord a bill.

Who pays household bills in my rental?

Who looks after the energy or broadband can vary, so check with your landlord when you sign your tenancy. If it is the tenant's responsibility then don't make the common mistake of assuming that you have to be on the energy tariff that is already in place. You can switch your provider to whoever you want, and in fact you should do this, because it could save you several hundred pounds.

When you move in, ask previous tenants or the landlord who is the current supplier. If no one knows, you can call a meter number helpline to find out who supplies gas on 0870 608 1524, and one of several numbers, depending on where you live, for electricity; the energy-uk.org.uk website has details. Take a meter reading at your new property as soon as you arrive. Tell the existing supplier that you've moved in and give the meter reading, so that you are not held liable for previous tenants' bills. You are responsible for any energy used when you take over the property, not just when you actually move in.

You will probably be put on the supplier's most expensive standard variable rate (more about this in the bills chapter 9), so you want to move off that as soon as possible. If you find a company that is cheaper just sign up and they will take care of contacting the old one and moving your supply. Do not forget to let them know, and take meter readings, when you move out.

2
How to buy a home

I will start off the tips in this chapter by saying that there is no magic solution to how difficult it is to afford a home where you want one. Apologies: you need more money. The options are limited: get a better-paid job, or a job somewhere with cheaper housing; beg and borrow from rich enough parents, friends, partners, perhaps with a boost from a family mortgage or a government scheme – read on for more; or start saving harder for longer (I hope that this book will help a bit with that).

Understanding the process of buying a home can, however, contribute towards working out whether you want or can stretch yourself to get on the ladder, and it can save you a lot of money on the stressful journey if or when the time eventually comes. **The experts suggest you get started thinking about how to make yourself a model homebuyer at least six months before you start engaging estate agents and banks. Don't panic if you do not have six months, it is possible to put yourself in a better position within weeks.**

Of those I know who have bought their first homes, many because the bank of Mum and Dad has chipped in, all have told a similar story: 'I had no idea what I was doing, so I felt like I was being totally shafted.'

The nature of the buying and selling process, which is a game of holding your nerve and outguessing who is trying to outmanoeuvre who, plus dealing with estate agents (a profession on equal pegging with journalists for the most able to put a creative spin on the truth), means that some shafting is hard to avoid. Steel yourself. But getting your head round the following should at least keep it to a minimum.

I will start by explaining the basics of how you can borrow money to buy a house, and then move on to the finer details of what mortgage to choose, plus all the other costs of the process, if by that point you reckon you can indeed raise the funds required.

First – what actually is a mortgage?

How to borrow enough to buy a property

Whether or not you can afford to buy the house you want boils down to two things: can you raise a big enough deposit, and can you borrow enough, given your earnings, outgoings and spending habits, to get a big enough mortgage to top up that deposit? We are going on the assumption here that you are not buying a house with a suitcase of cash: if you are under forty and do not need a mortgage you do not need this book.

When working out the size of the deposit you can save, don't forget that there are lots of other expenses involved in buying a house that you need to budget for – for example, stamp duty, which can be tens of thousands of pounds on expensive properties, and solicitors' fees. Skip to later in the chapter for an estimation of how much these will cost you.

How your deposit influences the mortgage you can get

The bigger your deposit, that is the lump sum of cash you are bringing to the party, the smaller the amount you have to borrow from a bank, the more of your property you actually 'own' from the start, and, naturally, the cheaper your monthly mortgage repayments.

Your monthly mortgage repayments will depend on the type of mortgage product you go for (read on for a detailed explanation of this), but will mostly likely consist of some capital repayment, that is an amount you pay to chip away at the fundamental sum that you are borrowing, and interest, which is, to put it most simply, the fee or the penalty you pay to borrow the money from the bank. Interest is charged as a percentage of the size of your mortgage, so if you borrowed £100,000 and your interest rate was 2 per cent, you would owe £2,000 interest a year, paid in monthly chunks.

The size of your mortgage is the size of the proportion of your property that the bank still technically 'owns'. If you can't pay your mortgage back your property will be repossessed, which means that the bank sells it to recover the value in cash of this proportion. If it is repossessed at a time when property prices are depressed and your home sells for less than you bought it at, you could end up owing the bank more money than you started with.

The aim is to pay down your mortgage over time and start to own more of your property. If house prices rise your house is worth more, so the amount of loan you have outstanding on it has shrunk relative to its value, though you will not feel the cash benefits of this unless you sell, or remortgage.

If house prices tumble, as happened after the financial crash, you could end up in 'negative equity', that is where you owe the bank more in a mortgage than your house is actually worth, and you will not be able to move, becoming what is known as a 'mortgage prisoner'. Falling into negative equity is less likely than it was, because since the credit crunch banks are much more cautious about how much money they will lend to you.

What is LTV?

The amount you can borrow in a mortgage is measured in a 'loan-to-value' rate, or LTV, as you will see on mortgage adverts. This is just the percentage mix of deposit and loan. If you had £20,000 cash and wanted to buy a £200,000 house, you would have a 10 per cent deposit, and need to borrow the remaining £180,000 to get your hands on it. That is you need to borrow 90 per cent of the property's value, or 90 per cent LTV. If you had £180,000 cash and needed to

borrow only £20,000 you would have a 90 per cent deposit, and would apply for a 10 per cent LTV mortgage.

Before the Crash it was common to see 100 per cent LTV mortgages. Northern Rock used to have 125 per cent LTV mortgages, which it scrapped in 2008. These existed because there was such general confidence that house prices were on a permanent climb. Banks are no longer so sanguine, though higher LTV loans have been creeping back onto the market aimed at first-time buyers.

There is a common rule in money matters that the higher the risk the higher the reward (see chapter on the stock market for more on this). If banks are taking a greater risk on you, stumping up £180,000 to lend to you rather than just £20,000, they want more of a reward, so you'll pay more on top of the sum you want to borrow, generally in the form of interest.

The greater your deposit, the cheaper your mortgage will be

This leads us on to another cruelty for first-time buyers struggling with the cost of housing: all the cheapest mortgage deals with the lowest interest rates are available to the borrowers that banks want the most: those who can save the biggest deposits. All the record-breaking low-interest-rate deals plastered over billboards are generally only given to those borrowing with an LTV of 65 per cent or less, or put the other way, who can contribute a deposit of at least 35 per cent of the cost of the property they want to buy.

Most first-time buyers, especially those buying a flat in an expensive city, will be looking at borrowing with a 5 per cent deposit, or 95 per cent LTV mortgage, or 10 per cent deposit and 90 per cent LTV mortgage.

• TOP TIP

If you can push yourself to find a 10 per cent deposit, you should. There is a particularly large interest-rate jump between mortgages offered to those with a 5 per cent deposit and those available to those with 10 per cent deposit. This can work out as, for example, £1000 more a year on a mortgage of just £100,000 brokers tell me.

How your bank is judging you

The deposit is most of the battle, but once you have scraped it together you will need to persuade a bank to lend you the rest, and that is a harder and more mysterious process than it used to be. For our parents it was as simple as telling a bank how much they earned. You could borrow a multiple of this. Now, while earnings count, they are not conclusive. Outgoings count just as much. Remember that banks are worried about taking a risk on you, especially when you are a first-timer, so will make all sorts of judgements on your spending pattern to check how safe a bet they can make that you will continue to pay off your mortgage each month.

They do this through looking at your credit score (more on how this works shortly) and your spending patterns, based on analysing bank statements, any debt you are in, and any regular expensive commitments that look fixed, such as a child, dog, Camel Lights habit etc. Your prospective lender will probably want to see at least the last three months of bank statements, as well as payslips, so collect these well in advance and make sure that within this period you do not exceed your overdraft limit or have any bounced payments.

Ray Boulger, of mortgage brokers John Charcol, says you should also bear in mind that a lender will be able to see who you are paying money to, 'so don't spend on things you think a lender might disapprove of' – bouts of online gambling, for example. Also he says give careful thought to signing up to Open Banking; this will allow a lender to see a longer spending history. (See budgeting chapter for more on open banking.)

You will also have to fill out an application form, detailing your outgoings. If this, or your bank statements, disclose lifestyle choices that make you look like a mega-spender, above-average numbers of holidays or meals out, say, that may reduce the amount you can borrow. The same goes if you have lots of financial debt commitments – such as car finance, personal loans or credit-card debt that you don't repay in full each month. As long as the debt is not judged excessive, though, it is the amount you are paying in monthly payments, and so reducing what is left to spend, that influences the amount you can borrow, not the outstanding debt. Debt with less than six months to run is usually ignored.

Student loans count only in so far as repaying them means you have less disposable income

**left in your bank account, which feeds into
how much you can afford to borrow. The fact
that you have student-loan 'debt' does not count
against you.**

Banks will also look to see how your income or
affordability levels may change in future. This is
why a former colleague of mine went to the bank to
apply for a mortgage with a very baggy top on, and
took good care to pay for any Mothercare purchases
with cash. If they had known she was going to have
a baby, she guessed they would have judged her on
balance a greater risk, likely to see both a dip in her
earnings and a rise in her outgoings, even though
she was pretty confident she could afford a big
mortgage just fine.

SIDENOTE It is illegal for a bank to discriminate
against an applicant because she is pregnant, so,
like a job interviewer, you cannot be asked: 'Are you
pregnant or do you plan to get pregnant?' But most
will have questions on their application forms like:
'Do you anticipate any changes to your financial
circumstances in the next three months which might
make it difficult for you to make your mortgage
payments?'

You need to be honest. Lying on the application form is fraud, though you do not have to disclose your pregnancy. It should, however, make you think hard about whether you can actually afford the mortgage you want if your income or circumstances change once you have got it. A bank can only know so much about your ability to repay in the future; it is up to you to gauge how much you want to stretch yourself, knowing what life or job changes lie ahead.

Earnings matter, if only to work out whether you stand a chance of buying

Before you start browsing Zoopla it is a good idea to work out roughly how much you are realistically going to be able to borrow based on your earnings. This is only part of the picture as explained above, but a good place to begin. There are lots of mortgage calculators online that work on this basis. **The rough rule of thumb at the moment, though it varies between banks, is that you can borrow about four to four and a half times your pre-tax salary. Some lenders will stretch to five times your salary, as long as it is affordable (if you are self-employed this might not apply – more below).**

Clydesdale bank this year launched a 'professional mortgage' with a maximum loan 5.5 times salaries if you are a newly qualified professional such as a doctor, vet, solicitor or architect. This is called an 'income multiple'. That means if you earn £35,000 a year before tax you are unlikely to be able to borrow more than about £158,000 if you are buying alone. Now you can see why there's a housing-affordability problem.

It is worth noting that the income multiple is the same for couples as for single applicants, so you are in a much stronger position if you buy with another person. Banks also treat 'non-guaranteed' income differently – items like commission payments and bonuses. This means you might get quirks where one bank actually offers you a bigger mortgage on a four-times-income multiple than another bank which is prepared to lend on a four-and-a-half-times-income multiple but does not allow for bonuses.

The maximum income multiple also varies with what LTV you can afford. Someone with a 25 per cent deposit is more likely to be able to borrow five times their income, whereas if you have just 5 per cent deposit, the maximum is unlikely to be more than four times. This maximum may also vary according to how much you earn, on the basis that you can allocate a higher proportion of your income to the mortgage repayments if you are richer. As Mr Boulger puts it: 'Someone earning £80,000 won't spend four times as much on toilet rolls as someone earning £20,000.'

How to get a mortgage if you are self-employed

You used to be able to apply for 'self-cert' mortgages, nicknamed 'liar loans', which allowed you, as a self-employed worker, to state your income without any actual proof of it. These were banned in 2014. If you are self-employed or a freelancer you apply for mortgages in the same ways as everyone else, but it is now a lot harder to get one, though do not give up before you have tried.

Ideally you need at least two years of accounts, and three years will go down even better. Many banks want these signed off by an accountant. You also need to show the income you have reported in your self-assessment tax return to HMRC; you can download the SA302 form and tax-year overview from HMRC's website.

Some lenders – for example, Halifax (if you have a great credit score), Newcastle Building Society, Kensington and Precise Mortgages – will consider those who have been self-employed for only a year. Smaller building societies tend to be a better bet: they are less likely to pull 'Computer says no'. You may also find it easier if you were with the same business as a full-time employee before you started going freelance.

If your earnings have been rising, banks will usually take your average income for the past two or so years. If it has fallen, they will probably use the latest and lowest figure of earnings. The best thing to do is apply to a lender you know will be most happy to offer you a deal given your specific circumstances. A broker can help matchmake. If you are self-employed, take extra care with spending in the run-up to a mortgage application. You want to act especially frugally for at least six months beforehand.

What is 'stress testing' and why the future matters as much as the present

Post-credit-crunch lending rules now also require banks to make sure that a mortgage is affordable not only right now but also in the future. **The result is 'stress testing'. You may be able to comfortably meet mortgage repayments on your existing salary with current low interest rates, but what if interest rates rise? You will only be able to borrow as much as you can happily afford with an interest rate of 3 per cent higher than it is today, usually compared with a bank's standard variable rate (more on what that is in a minute) at the point at which you apply. That means most first-time buyers are stress-tested on the basis of a mortgage that might fall payable with interest of 7 to 7.5 per cent.**

This protects you from overstretching yourself, but also means you are limited with how great a risk you can take on borrowing, even if you feel confident that your earnings are going to increase significantly in the future.

What is your credit score and why does it matter?

When it assesses whether or not you can afford a mortgage, a bank will score your creditworthiness based on information it can gather from your credit history or credit file as well as your bank statements. Your credit history is a record of your interactions with other financial companies: banks, energy providers and so on, kept by credit-reference agencies. Your prospective lender is looking for evidence of past borrowing behaviour to assess whether or not you will be a well-behaved borrower going forward.

You are also judged on things like how long you have been with the same employer, how long you have lived at your address, and how long you have had your bank account.

Most banks, building societies and financial companies have their own arcane bespoke credit-scoring system, based on what factors they deem important as a yardstick of reliability. No one is quite sure how they all work, how they are compiled, and how banks use them. Underwriters at banks, that is the team that assess risk, will not reveal how they compile and assess credit scores because they are 'commercially sensitive', so you can be rejected for having, in their view, a bad score, without knowing why, or being able to argue that their criteria are wrong.

You do not have one single credit score – this is a myth – but UK banks use three credit-reference agencies in the UK for information: Experian, Equifax and Callcredit. They compile their own credit scores based on their own assessment of your credit history, and you can check them to get some idea of whether or not you look like a worthy borrower. They are useful, but just guidelines.

Despite their opaque nature, credit scores are annoyingly important, and used for everything from overdrafts and credit cards to mobile-phone deals and, crucially, mortgages. I have received letters in my role as consumer champion at *The Times* from people on the verge of losing a house they want, or unable to secure an affordable mortgage, because of minor bill infractions or disputes, like forgetting to clear a small sum owed to an energy company on an account for a shared flat after everyone moves out, or missing a mobile-phone payment. These have resulted in letters from debt collectors, which damaged the reader's credit history.

One man thought his gas account had been put on hold over a bill he did not think he owed while it was investigated; instead it had been passed to debt collectors, and a 'late-payment' notice added to his credit report. As a result he was turned down for a cheaper mortgage, and estimated that it would cost him over £10,000 more.

One first-time buyer couple applied for three new bank accounts – a current account each, and a joint account with the same bank that had agreed to lend them a mortgage – because they were told it would simplify things. Instead their credit score was damaged by the fact that they applied for too many financial products at once, even though the bank was getting more of their business. Totally bizarre, but really expensive, they could no longer apply for a 95 per cent LTV mortgage; they had to find another £12,000 for a deposit for a 90 per cent one. Luckily their grandparents bailed them out, but others less fortunate would have lost the house.

How to improve your credit history

If you were going to lend someone several hundred thousand pounds you would want to know a bit about how likely they were to pay you back, based on how well they had paid other people back in the past. You might be equally reluctant to lend to them if you had no evidence of their reliability because they had never borrowed from anyone before. **What people do not realize is that although debt is portrayed as something you should generally avoid, having no credit history is as bad as having a faulty one. Banks need something to go on.** This can be a problem for young first-time buyers whose only experience of financial products is their bank account and children's saver they signed up to when they were twelve, or for people moving here from abroad who leave their credit histories behind in another country.

What it is useful to do, ideally at least six months before you apply for a mortgage, is create a wholesome credit portrait of yourself and, if you have no credit history, start borrowing small amounts to build one up. Start by checking your credit record through one or all of the three main credit-reference agencies mentioned above: Equifax, Experian and Callcredit. You can do this free, though be warned that you only get it free by signing up for a free trial period, after which you start to get charged automatically. Many people are caught out by this, so unsubscribe as soon as you have your score. Noddle lets you check your Callcredit score and is 'free for life'.

I recommend that you check the credit-reference agencies at least six months before you start to apply for a mortgage, so that you have time to sort it out if it's poor, but it's worth doing even if you intend to apply for a mortgage next week.

• MAKE SURE YOU ARE ON THE ELECTORAL ROLL

This is essential. If you are not you won't get a mortgage. Banks use the electoral roll to check you are who you say you are. Make sure your name is spelled right, all your address history is correct and up to date, and that you are registered to vote at the same, most recent, address.

• GET A CREDIT CARD AND USE IT IN A CHILLED-OUT MANNER

If you have a poor score because you have not had credit in the past, take out a credit card and use it for day-to-day shopping for a few months. Set up a direct debit to clear if off in full every month. Don't just pay the minimum payment, but don't max it out either: the perfect amount of spending is about 10 to 30 per cent of your credit-card limit. It demonstrates that you can borrow sensibly without losing the plot with all this lovely free money. A monthly credit-card balance below 30 per cent can gain you 90 points on your credit score, according to Experian, which scores from 0 to 999. A score of around 780 is fair, one of above 961 or higher is excellent. A card balance above 90 per cent will cost you 50 points.

• ADD RENT TO YOUR CREDIT HISTORY

You can now ask for rental payments to be added to your Experian credit score to demonstrate that you are a reliable rent-payer. Not all banks take this into account yet, but there are hopes that this will slowly start to change, so it is worth doing.

The Rental Exchange scheme records your rental payments and sends the results to Experian. You need to actively sign up to do this by paying your rent through a company called Credit Ladder, which then passes on your money to your landlord or letting agent, so run this past your landlord to check that they are happy with it first. Equifax and Callcredit don't yet consider rental payments.

• DON'T APPLY FOR OTHER STUFF

Don't be over-keen. Applying for too many accounts and loans in a short space of time does not go down well. If you can, avoid applying for anything (mobile phone, credit card, bank account) within six months or so of applying for your mortgage.

• BREAK UP WITH YOUR EX

Break any links to ex-partners and former flatmates with whom you have shared joint accounts or joint bills. If you are still wrongly linked on your report, contact all three agencies to ask them for a 'disassociation'. Contrary to popular belief, just living with someone else who failed to pay their bills on time will not damage your credit file, but if you were financially tied to them then their poor credit history will reflect negatively on yours (conversely their excellent credit history reflects well on you). Bear this in mind before you open any kind of joint financial product.

• PAY ALL YOUR BILLS ON TIME

Make sure you do not default on any household bills. Credit reports include information from, for example, your gas, electricity, insurance and water supplier. Any defaults, even if you failed to pay just £5, stay on and damage your report for six years.

Missing your last payment on an account will cost you about 130 points according to Experian; receiving a default, when an account is passed to debt collectors, or getting a court judgement, will cost you more than 250 points. These things fade over time, though: after three years you will lose fewer points for them. If there are any mistakes on your report, or any defaults that you think are unfair or misrepresent you, then you can ask the credit-reference agency to investigate them and add a note of up to 200 words (known as a notice of correction) on your file to put them right. Lay out why you feel they are unfair, or why your circumstances have changed. For example, you might write that you missed a bill because you had lost your job, but you are now fully employed and back to paying bills on time.

• REDUCE YOUR DEBTS (BUT DON'T WORRY ABOUT STUDENT LOANS)

Pay down any debt you have as much as possible before applying for a mortgage: lenders will look at your 'balance trend' as part of credit scoring. This does not include student loans. Arguably you would be better off boosting your deposit than using savings to pay down any student loan. See the next chapter for more on why.

• BE CAREFUL ON FACEBOOK

There have been stories that banks take what you post on social media into account. This is hard to prove, but Andrew Montlake, of the mortgage broker Coreco, told me that he would suggest those looking to apply for a mortgage should be careful about what they share. 'Gambling stories, wild nights out and lavish spending boasts should probably be avoided.' Also avoid sending or receiving cash to your bank with 'banterous' references. Banks have rejected people based on 'drug money' appearing on their statements, even if it is obviously a joke.

• DO NOT GET A PAYDAY LOAN

For some banks payday loans are also an absolute credit-score killer. Some banks will not lend to you at all if you have taken out a payday loan, others are less fussed. But best not to go anywhere near Wonga at least a year before you apply for a mortgage if you can help it. Ideally never go anywhere near Wonga.

• GET A COPY OF YOUR OLD REPORT IF YOU HAVE MOVED TO THE UK FROM ABROAD

If you have moved from abroad, bring a copy of your credit record from the main agency in your home country to the UK, then contact Experian, Equifax and Callcredit and ask them to put a note on your file that you are willing to provide a copy of your credit history. Monese offers bank accounts to people who have no proof of address, maybe because they have no credit record in the UK and therefore their name is not on a utility bill.

You have got a deposit and can afford a mortgage! So what is the process of buying a house?

You spot a house you like advertised with an estate agent. You work out whether you can afford it and stamp duty based on whether you can get a mortgage. You can at this stage get a 'mortgage in principle', which is a non-binding agreement stating how much, based on your income, outgoings and credit score, a bank will lend you. If all looks good, you put in an offer for the property, which is hopefully accepted by the seller. You then appoint a property lawyer to start what is called the conveyancing process. You find the mortgage you want – it doesn't have to be with the same bank that gave you a mortgage in principle – and apply for it for real.

Once the sellers have accepted your offer there is still no guarantee that they will definitely sell to you, just a 'gentleman's agreement'. There is a chance that you could get gazumped. That's where another seller swoops in with a higher offer, and a greedy seller dumps you for the new bidders. Gazundering is where you, the buyer, lower your offer just before exchange of contracts. There is nothing other than your conscience, and the risk of pissing off the seller, who may pull out, to stop you doing this, but all the same, better not to – bad karma.

Cross your fingers you do not get gazumped, and insist that the person you are buying from takes down the online or estate-agent advert for their home (the estate agent probably will not do this unless you force them to). In Scotland an offer being accepted is legally binding, sometimes subject to a mortgage being approved, so you are unlikely to be gazumped, or pull out once you have put your offer in.

Your bank will carry out affordability and credit-score checks and then, with a mortgage-valuation survey, on the property you want to buy. This survey is not the same as a building survey, which checks whether the house is in good condition. You need to set this up yourself.

Meanwhile your solicitor will be carrying out checks too, on things like whether your property is on a floodplain. You have to pay for these. Press your solicitor for these to be completed quickly.

When you have received your mortgage offer and your solicitor is ready you can exchange contracts, a process carried out between your own and the seller's solicitor. At this stage you normally need to pay 10 per cent – sometimes, if you negotiate, 5 per cent – of the price of the property you are buying to your solicitor, who passes it on to the seller's solicitor. Make sure you have this money ready to be transferred out of your bank account; some banks will require a few days' notice.

Be super-careful about the accuracy of your solicitor's bank details. There is a common fraud where solicitors' email accounts are hacked by a fraudster who sends out an email to a buyer

stating that the solicitor's bank details have changed, or adding in false sort codes and account numbers. If in any doubt, call your solicitor to check again where you send the money. Once you've clicked send it's gone, and you cannot get it back if you send it to the wrong place. I've seen this happen several times, and it is heartbreaking.

You also need, at this stage, to arrange buildings insurance, legally required as part of receiving a mortgage.

You agree a day of completion, on which you arrange to send over the rest of your home deposit, plus any fees owed to your solicitor, as well as stamp duty. Your solicitor will receive cash from your mortgage company and arrange to send this to the seller's solicitor on completion day, at which point you receive the keys for your new home. Woohoo!

The many other costs of buying a house

When working out whether you can afford to buy you need to budget for all the many other unexpected costs that crop up along the way: stamp duty, legal costs, local authority searches, survey costs, mortgage arrangement fees, mortgage broker fees, buildings insurance, removal vans, and, only if you are selling too, estate-agency fees.

Need-to-knows: Stamp duty

This is the biggest cost of moving, a tax you pay on any property you buy in the UK. The tax is based on the price of the property you are buying, and is staggered in thresholds. For example, you pay 2 per cent of a property's value on properties priced between £125,001 and £250,000; 5 per cent on properties worth between £250,001 and £925,000; 10 per cent on properties worth £925,001 to £1.5 million.

First-time buyers are exempt from paying stamp duty on any home worth below £300,000. If the property you want to buy is worth more than £300,000 but less than £500,000 you pay 5 per cent of any proportion between the two.

If you are buying with another person you both have to be first-time buyers, otherwise it does not count. There is an exception if only one person's name is on the deeds, and that person is a first-time buyer, but only if you are not married. You are not a first-time buyer if you have already owned a property in another country, or if you have inherited a property. You also only get the exemption if you are buying a home to live in. It does not apply to buy to let, even if you have never bought a property before.

Conveyancing

You need a property solicitor or conveyancer to help you buy a house. Expect to pay fees in the region of £1,000 to £1,500. Having a solicitor who cracks on with the work and will answer your calls promptly will save you a lot of aggro, so a personal recommendation is probably the best way to find one. Failing that, The Law Society website's 'find a solicitor' section lists conveyancers. You do not need to use a local solicitor. You could find a more affordable, reliable one from back home, even if you are buying in London, for example.

You will also need to pay your solicitor certain fees for Land Registry, which charges for changing the ownership of a home into your name, and local authority searches. Budget an additional £300 or so.

Finding a solicitor before you put in a house offer makes you look organized and committed and can help save precious time when an offer has been accepted and you want to exchange as soon as possible.

Surveys

When you get a mortgage your bank will want to check that the property you want to buy actually exists, as well as that it is worth the price you are going to pay for it: the bank does not want to lose money if it has to repossess. It will therefore carry out a mortgage-valuation survey, which you will probably have to pay for: a few hundred pounds. Do not make the frequently made mistake of relying on this as some kind of comprehensive survey of whether or not the house you are buying may fall down.

You need another building survey, by a qualified surveyor, or the less extensive homebuyer's survey to check for damp or rot or Japanese knotweed or a ceiling that is about to collapse. You are not obliged to have one, but you may regret it if you do not and there are extensive problems in your new home.

Some are considered not worth the paper they are written on, however, so put some research into what kind of survey to go for, and whether it is worth it for the type of property you are buying. Expect to pay from £300 to well over £1,000, according to the HomeOwners Alliance. The Royal Institution of Chartered Surveyors site (RICS.org) is a good starting point.

Mortgage brokers

First-time buyers will particularly benefit from using an independent mortgage broker or mortgage adviser who can help you wade through the different mortgage products that are out there. Brokers can also hurry along a lender and keep things progressing smoothly, filling out all application forms for you. Some brokers charge fees of from £300 to several thousand, others get commission from banks they match up to borrowers, either instead of or as well as a fee.

Broker London & Country does not charge a fee and promises that, though it gets commission, you do not get any worse a mortgage deal than you would if you went to the bank directly.

Do not be bullied into using an estate agent's preferred adviser. You are under absolutely no obligation to meet their 'in-house broker', and it is illegal for estate agents to suggest that the price of the house you want to buy will go up unless you do. A word-of-mouth recommendation is often best, or you can search the website unbiased.co.uk for regulated advisers.

Brokers will try to recommend add-on products while arranging your mortgage – life insurance for example. You will find a better deal by searching elsewhere, so don't feel pressured by any hard sell (see chapter 9 for more on this).

Choosing a mortgage

What's actually in a mortgage?

A mortgage is likely to be your biggest financial outlay for the next twenty to thirty years. Choose wisely and you save thousands of pounds. There are a lot of mortgages to choose from, however, so it's not easy. A broker will help you navigate the market, but first understand what you are signing up for yourself.

How much a mortgage will cost you up front, when you first get accepted for one, and from month to month for the next few years, depends on what that mortgage 'product' is made up of and the length of its term. Most are a mix of capital repayment, interest, and arrangement fees. These fees are significant, sometimes several thousand pounds.

The 'term' is how long a period you are given to pay back your mortgage. Many are twenty-five years, though the first forty-year mortgages have started to appear. You can lower the amount you pay month on month by opting for a longer term, but longer terms accrue more interest over time. It is a balancing act.

Similarly a mortgage with the cheapest interest rate is not always the cheapest deal over the longer term. You need to work out whether lower arrangement fees mean that you may be better off with a slightly higher interest rate, or vice versa. Banks are clever at making an offer look more attractive with low advertised rates but ultra-high arrangement fees.

Also look out for flexibility. Can you overpay your mortgage without being charged fees if you expect a bumper pay rise in the future? Can you take any break from mortgage payments without penalty if, for example, you know there's a period when you will see a dip in earnings?

Should you get a fixed-rate or a tracker mortgage?

• BUT FIRST, WHAT IS THE BASE RATE?

The base rate is the national interest rate set by the Bank of England, and it is to the base rate that high-street banks and building societies peg their mortgage rates (as well as their savings rates, see chapter 5).

Following the Crash, the base rate was cut to a historic low of just 0.5 per cent, where it stayed until 2016, when it fell even further to 0.25 per cent. Low interest rates can help to revive the economy, they are good for businesses – borrowing is cheaper – and should make citizens spend rather than save. It is rising at the moment slightly, but is still at record lows. Young first-time buyers have never known anything other than cheap interest rates on mortgages, but it may not always be this way. In

1990, the base rate was nearly 15 per cent, in 1980 it was 17 per cent.

Variable rates, pros and cons

When choosing a mortgage one of the biggest decisions is whether to get a variable rate, a tracker-rate mortgage or a fixed-rate mortgage.

A variable rate is fairly self-explanatory. The mortgage lender sets the price of its variable rate and may at any point raise it or lower it; variable rates will rise when the base rate rises, but banks may set them as they like. **All lenders will have a 'standard variable rate' (SVR), which is their default product that you will revert to whenever the special deal you might sign up for, say a two-year tracker, ends.**

The SVR is usually more expensive than the best mortgage deals on the market, so it pays not to sit on it for any length of time, though many people do. Recent research by mortgage broker Dynamo suggested that a third of people whose mortgage deal expired in 2017 spent forty-two days on the SVR, which cost an average of £371 more than they needed to be paying, in 'procrastination penalty'.

A tracker rate is a variable-rate mortgage, but one that is actually pegged to the base rate. So for example you might have a tracker-rate mortgage of 1.99 per cent, which would work out at an interest rate of 2.49 per cent when the base rate is at 0.5 per cent, and rise to 2.99 per cent if the base rate rose to 1 per cent.

The cost of your mortgage rises proportionally with the base rate. You can sign up to a tracker with various different lengths: a lifetime tracker runs for the full term of your mortgage, say twenty-five years, or you could have a two-, three-, five- or ten-year tracker.

Fixed rates pros and cons

Fixed rates do not alter with the base rate. You lock into a specific rate for a set period – two, three or five years normally, but increasingly ten-year fixed rates have come onto the market. Whether you go for a variable or a fixed rate comes down to how much you want to bet on base rates rising or falling. Fixed rates are best for people who want the certainty of knowing exactly how much they must pay month by month for their mortgage for the next few years, but they may be slightly more expensive. You need to make a clear-eyed decision, because you will pay high exit fees to get out of your deal, whether it is fixed or tracker: as much as 5 per cent of your mortgage in what is known as an early repayment charge (ERC).

You may also be charged an ERC for paying off a chunk of your mortgage at once, for example, if/when you win the lottery. Some deals let you overpay a certain percentage a year if you can afford to, but there is a limit.

When weighing up your options, consider that every time you move deal you will probably have to pay arrangement fees. If you are signing up for an inexpensive-seeming two-year deal, factor in that you will have to soon pay out arrangement fees when it comes to an end and you want a new rate.

On the other hand the downside of signing up for a deal that is very long, say a ten-year fix, is that you may struggle to transfer it to a new house if you intend to move. Some mortgage deals are 'portable', but if your circumstances have changed since you took it out, or your bank does not like the look of your new place, you may struggle.

Watch out for any small print that allows a bank to put up its tracker rates even when the base rate does not rise. Some have a 'collar' that stops your rate falling too low if the base rate falls below a certain minimum.

Buying with the Bank of Mum and Dad (BOMAD): top tips and family mortgages

The Bank of Mum and Dad became the UK's ninth-biggest unofficial mortgage lender, in 2017 helping to fund 26 per cent of all UK property transactions, on a par with Yorkshire Building Society, according to research by Legal & General. Of those under thirty-five seeking to buy in 2017, 62 per cent were being partially bankrolled by parents or other family members.

This has bred a new category of family mortgages. David Hollingworth, of broker London & Country, says you should not necessarily head straight for something badged up a first-time buyer deal – a normal mortgage might be cheaper or more appropriate. Nevertheless if you are struggling with a deposit there are some innovative solutions.

Barclays Family Springboard will lend as much as 100 per cent LTV as long as your parent will lock 10 per cent of the property price (i.e. the 10 per cent deposit they might otherwise have given you) in cash into a linked savings account as additional security. This means your parent keeps their cash in their name rather than giving it to you, and will be able to access it at a later date, within three years, assuming you make all your mortgage payments on time.

Post Office's Family Link gives you the opportunity to take out two mortgages on two properties, 90 per cent LTV on the one you want to buy and 10 per cent against your parents' home. You the buyer pay off both loans, but the 10 per cent one is interest-free, though you have to clear it within five years. You must be a first-time buyer to take advantage of this, and your parents must have an income of at least £20,000.

Aldermore has a similar concept, a Family Guarantee mortgage, again at 100 per cent LTV, which allows parents to use spare equity in their own home as security, rather than cash, as do Family Building Society and Bath Building Society. The major drawback of these is that your parents' home is at risk of being repossessed if you cannot pay your mortgage, which could make for some tense Sunday lunches. They are also more expensive than conventional mortgages. If your parents can afford to give you cash instead, you will get a better interest rate.

If your parents or grandparents are giving you some or all of your deposit in cash, lenders will want to know whether it is a gift or a loan, and whether the money has any strings attached, such as having to repay them monthly. This will affect the perceived affordability of your mortgage and therefore how much you can borrow. A 'soft loan', which is where your parents expect to be repaid, but only when you sell your property, therefore no monthly repayments are required, is not a problem. Banks will often require a letter from your parents confirming that the money is a gift, or a 'soft loan'.

First-time buyer schemes to help you buy (with or without BOMAD)

You can take advantage of the following options whether or not you have money from your parents. If you are saving up to buy your first home use either a Lifetime ISA or Help to Buy ISA and you get some free cash from the government. See more details in savings chapter 5.

Help to Buy Equity loan

This government scheme has been extended to run until 2021. The idea is to help those with small deposits to access bigger homes and better interest rates. By its terms, you have to buy a new-build property from an approved house builder, with a 5 per cent deposit, receiving a 20 per cent loan from the government. This means you can take out a 75 per cent LTV mortgage; those buying in London receive a 40 per cent loan, so they need borrow only 60 per cent LTV.

The 20 per cent loan is interest-free for the first five years, then you have to pay interest at initially 1.75 per cent, a rate which increases in line with CPI inflation (for more on what that is, see the savings chapter 5). In exchange, the government, like the bank, owns 20 per cent of your property. You pay this off if and when you move, or you can pay it off sooner if you have managed to save the money.

Your mortgage should be a lot more affordable because you have a lower LTV despite your small 5 per cent deposit. Typically monthly payments are reduced by a third compared with what you would be paying with a 95 per cent LTV. As a result many first-time buyers using Help to Buy have been able to afford a slightly bigger property. There is a limit on how much you can pay for your home. In England this is £600,000, in Wales, £300,000. In Scotland £200,000.

One of the downsides is, as some people who took out their Help to Buy loans five years ago are now finding, that if your property does not appreciate in price much you may struggle to repay the government stake and buy another home. If you sell you may find that you have gained little. Many will sign up for Help to Buy assuming that they will use the increased value of their property to remortgage and pay off the equity loan. There are also complaints that those who come to the end of their original Help to Buy mortgage term may struggle to remortgage on to a better deal; there are fewer Help to Buy eligible remortgage products available.

You can find more details on the Help to Buy website (helptobuy.org.uk).

Shared ownership

If you cannot afford a whole property you can actually buy part of one, from just 25 per cent of it to 75 per cent of it, through the shared-ownership scheme. You rent the rest from a housing association, as long as you earn less than £80,000, or if you are buying in London, £90,000. This is per household though, so combined income if you are a couple. You can search for eligible properties on sharetobuy.com.

Take a three-bedroom flat available in Cambridge. Its full price is £415,000 but you can buy a 30 per cent share in it for £124,500, which requires a mortgage deposit of just £6,225. Your monthly cost would be £1,407, made up of a £624 a month mortgage, rent of £666 and a service charge of £117. Sounds like just the solution, but there are a lot of catches with shared ownership, so do your research to see if it actually suits you.

First, that massive service charge. Though you own only, say, 30 per cent, you have to pay 100 per cent of the service charge, which is a monthly charge you pay the housing association for maintenance. Service charges are infamously expensive, and notorious for rising steeply. Likewise, rents on the proportion you do not own may also rise and become less affordable, though rents are less than would be charged on the open market – usually 2.75 per cent of the property value per year. You can start to buy more shares in the property, up to 100 per cent of the whole thing, in a process known as staircasing, but again, if property values rise you may not be able to afford to do this. Also you may be limited to how many times you can 'staircase', so you couldn't for example buy just 1 per cent each year.

Shared-ownership mortgages come with higher interest rates than conventional mortgages. There are also certain restrictions on what you can do with your home because, really, you are still considered a tenant. You cannot sublet it, for example, which makes life a bit difficult if you have to move elsewhere for work. If you fall behind on rent there is the risk you will lose the property.

You can always sell and realize any gain you have made on the portion you own, supposing that house prices have risen, but the housing association has a right to find a buyer before you sell through the open market.

3

The debt you are in and how to handle it

Debt is a dirty word, so much so that a long time back the financial services industry rebranded it as the much more enticing 'credit'. But although many of us often called 'generation debt' are up to our eyeballs in it, not all debt is created equal, or owed equally urgently. You should not unnecessarily freak yourself out about borrowing money to the detriment of its many positive benefits (your own flat, university degree, iPhone, car, good credit score) or of getting a decent night's sleep.

Wrapping your head round how to borrow well is also one of the most efficient ways to avoid wasting money, which is why I think it is a topic worth addressing ahead of how best to budget, or start a savings account or pension. There is no point in having money set aside if you are paying out hundreds of pounds in interest on overdraft or credit-card debts because you have not managed to clear them quickly enough.

If you were to borrow £3,000 on a credit card, with an interest rate of 19 per cent (some credit cards now charge interest rates of over 50 per cent), and only make the minimum repayments, starting at £74 a month and reducing over time, it would take you twenty-seven years and seven

months to pay it off, and you would have paid an additional £4,192 in interest in the meantime, highlighted the Financial Conduct Authority, the financial services industry regulator. That £3,000 would have cost you £7,192. If you could stretch to repaying £108 a month, by not saving until the debt was cleared, for example, you would get rid of it in three years, and pay £879 in interest. The debt would have cost you £3,879.

I will come on to how best to have and use credit cards, but, having dealt with mortgages, I'll start with the second-biggest debt you are most likely to be juggling – a student loan. Ironically, that is the debt that should cause the least insomnia. I will then outline the debts that are far more pernicious, and how best to handle them in a way that helps you save money.

If you are mired in really messy debt with a bank or similar lender there are things you can do and people available to help you out of it, so please don't let it harm your mental health. I have covered this in chapter 11 on money and wellbeing.

Student loans

Putting aside all the controversial politics of whether or not students should have to pay tuition fees, and the rising cost of living at university, you have to admit that student loans have suffered from a shocking PR job. We have all read the news reports about bright young people being forced into £50,000 of 'debt' that they will be lumbered with for the whole of their twenties, thirties and forties, at least. While this is technically true, the implications are often misunderstood. The connotations of the dirty D word can be dangerously offputting, especially if you have grown up in a household stalked by debt, or cannot rely on BOMAD to bail you out.

What you need to remember is that with student-loan debt you will never need bailing out. You do not pay anything until you are independently well off enough to do so, whatever your parents' financial situation, and for anyone who has been to university since 1998 (unless you move abroad to live and forget to inform the SLC) no bailiffs will ever be involved. If you cannot meet your student-loan repayments you will not have

to pay them. You can borrow £50,000 and repay zero pounds if you are on minimum wage until your fifties. Martin Lewis, the money-saving expert, describes it as a sort of 'no win no fee' education, starving graduate artists and authors excepted.

Banks and payday loan companies, on the other hand, do not give a shit how much you earn. You owe them regardless of whether or not your salary dips, which is why people can get in such a sticky situation when they have borrowed far more than they can ever afford to repay. No win, even more massive fee.

The richest graduates, those that go into banking, City law firms, management consultancy and so on, and can more easily cover repayments, are the ones who will pay off the most, regardless of whether or not they came from a poor background. Obviously this is skewed by wealthy students who have parents that can afford to pay their tuition fees and living costs for them up front, but let's ignore that for the sake of understanding why you should try not to fear this kind of debt.

Also this is not necessarily the best use of BOMAD, for reasons outlined in the 'Should I repay my student loan early?' section below. If there is that much money sloshing about, they should probably gift you a house deposit instead.

I find it most helpful to think about student-loan debt as a tax, or as Martin Lewis calls it a 'graduate contribution', that you start paying only when you graduate, and only when you earn a certain amount of salary. CEOs do not lie awake at night in their Fulham pads worrying about how to pay additional-rate tax that is automatically deducted from their salary, though they will potentially owe millions over their lifetime, even if they are unhappy about that fact. Similarly, you should not lie awake worrying about how you will repay your student loan, even if you think it is deeply unfair that it exists.

Like the CEOs and their monumental tax bills, your student-loan repayment will reduce the amount of money you have in your bank account, which will have an impact on how much you can afford to spend on other already pretty unaffordable things like saving for a house. This reduction in income will also impact how much you may be able to borrow in a mortgage, but it will not spiral out of control to the point where you cannot pay it.

Those like me who graduated before 2012 will stop paying the tax sooner than those who started university after 2012, because we borrowed much less. In the short term though, the loans for us older graduates are actually more onerous, because the amount we have to earn before we start paying this 'tax' is lower (more details shortly).

What I think is particularly confusing is that interest rates on student loans are, for those younger students borrowing the most, largely irrelevant unless you are a high graduate earner (a City lawyer, one of those CEOs). They could go up to 5,000 per cent and under the current system it would make no difference for many graduates. This is, of course, dependent on a future government not completely changing the system, and no one can predict what may happen, but with the situation as it is now, here's why and what you actually have to pay.

Need to know: loans for students who started university after 2012, when tuition fees went up to £9,000

You will start repaying your loan only when you earn £25,000 or above before tax (prices true of

April 2018–2019), starting the April after you graduate. That £25,000 threshold will rise each year with RPI (a measure of inflation) or average earnings (see the savings chapter 5 for a fuller description of RPI for an explanation of what that means).

Your repayment is a fixed amount, like a tax: 9 per cent of everything you earn above the £25,000 threshold, regardless of interest rate charged on your loan. That means if you earn £26,000 you pay back £90 a year (£1,000 above the threshold, 9 per cent of £1,000 = £90). If you earn £35,000 you pay £900 a year (£10,000 above the threshold, 9 per cent of £10,000 = £900). You can see why higher earners pay more off, more quickly, because their 9 per cent is a much bigger sum. You can also see how much you will need to earn to make any substantial dent in £50,000. Especially because your loan is completely written off thirty years from the April after you graduate – for most undergraduates, when they hit their early fifties. That means an estimated 83 per cent, according to the Institute of Fiscal Studies, of post-2012 graduates will never pay back the full cost of their university days.

Interest is charged on your original loan. While you are studying this amounts to RPI + 3 per cent. It then changes. If you are earning under the repayment threshold, interest is pegged to RPI inflation. For those earning between the threshold and £45,000 it slowly rises in increments to RPI + 3 per cent for those earning £45,000 or above.

The fact that you accrue interest means that your loan will grow, which means it will take longer to pay it off. But most people will never pay it off in full within the thirty-year time frame anyway. However large your loan becomes – if it were to grow to £100,000 with interest – you still only pay off 9 per cent above the threshold each year. That is why unless you are earning a lot of money you don't need to worry too much about interest charged, because you only pay off what you can within thirty years.

If interest rises lots, fewer people will clear the loan within thirty years. Richer graduates will feel the pain, though, because they will be paying much more for longer than if the loan were interest-free.

Should I pay off my post-2012 student loan early?

I watched Martin Lewis give an impassioned speech about student loans to a bunch of students at King's College London in 2018, some of whom told him that they had indeed been worrying about how they could clear their student debt as quickly as possible, because of scary news reports. They did not really understand how the debt worked. He raised two real-life examples of people who had asked him the question of whether they should try and pay a bit off their outstanding loans, which I think explains it well.

The first people who asked him were parents of a girl who had to drop out of university because she was injured in an accident, is now severely disabled, and is unlikely ever to work. They were extremely worried about the debt she 'owed'. Should they repay her loan from her first year of studying? His answer was an emphatic no. She is unlikely to ever earn enough above the threshold to repay, the debt will be wiped after thirty years, any repayment will be money down the drain. They had no idea, because they had heard only the word 'debt', and had already spoken to the Student Loans Company to start to arrange repayments.

Another was a young graduate who had been offered a gift of £10,000 from her grandparents. Should she use it to pay her loan down? Again, probably not. This is because she is unlikely to ever pay the full loan back. If she reduced the debt to £40,000 from, for example, £50,000 and only just managed to clear the £40,000, she would have 'lost' the £10,000.

Now what if you expect to earn a lot of money? Presumably then it is worth trying to repay early?

Yes, possibly, because interest rates on the new post-2012 student loans are, controversially, much higher than some interest rates on other financial products such as mortgages and savings accounts, though it might be advisable if you have spare money to get on the housing ladder first, given how much you pay out in rent. It is not an exact science.

Martin Lewis suggests that only those who land a graduate job with a starting salary of £40,000, which then goes up with inflation and decent regular pay rises (no guarantee in this jobs market), should try to repay early to avoid mounting interest. Someone earning £36,000 on graduation, however, with their salary rising steadily with average earnings rise, will only repay

£40,500 of a £55,000 total student loan over thirty years.

This varies of course, because earnings sometimes jump later in life, or you might change careers . . . there are lots of factors. The Money Saving Expert site has a calculator where you can play with the sliders to see how likely you are to repay your full loan within thirty years.

Need to know: plan 1 student loans, for everyone who started university between 1998 and 2011, and Scottish and Northern Irish students who started after 2012

For those in their late twenties and thirties, like me, your student loan, known as a 'plan 1' type, looks different. You will start to repay your loan when you earn anything over £18,330 a year (in 2018–2019). That threshold usually rises each year.

Your repayment is also a fixed amount, 9 per cent, like a tax you pay on everything above £18,330 a year. So earn £20,000 and you will repay £150.30 a year (9 per cent of £1,670, the difference between £20,000 and £18,330 = £150.30);

£30,000 and it's £1,050.30 a year. Interest rates are lower than the new post-2012 English loans, currently (2018–2019) set at 1.5 per cent. Interest is calculated as either the Bank of England base rate plus 1 per cent, or the rate of RPI inflation whichever is lower.

Should I pay a plan 1 loan off early?

The answer is less obvious than for current students with ridiculous-sized loans, because most graduates will eventually clear their smaller pre-2012 student loans. You therefore have something to gain by doing so sooner, given that your loan is not totally interest-free. Nevertheless the interest rate is, at the moment, particularly low compared with other types of debt and finance, with less frightening repayment terms and consequences. You may find that it is less expensive to clear it at 9 per cent a year and use any disposable income or gift from BOMAD to save for a house deposit or pension, than to clear it and carry on struggling to make the rent. Certainly do not pay off your student loan before clearing other debts where high interest rates and bailiffs are involved.

Which leads us on to the scary types of debt.

Personal loans

If you need an injection of cash, to pay for a wedding, new car, new boiler, holiday, you might take out a personal loan. These are 'unsecured' loans, i.e. they are not tethered to anything like a house. A mortgage loan is 'secured' against your property: if you cannot pay the bank gets to sell your house as compensation.

If you cannot repay it, however, your debt may be passed on to a debt-collection agency. This is not the same as a bailiff – debt-collection agencies can only request that you repay a debt. Meanwhile interest charges may pile up, so that you eventually have to declare bankruptcy if you cannot pay. A bailiff can come to your property and remove your TV. Bailiffs will only tend to collect debts relating to things like council tax, parking fines or an unpaid TV licence.

Personal loans are more expensive than the best credit cards on the market, but you can usually borrow a bit more with a personal loan, so it depends why you need the cash. With a loan you will normally pay a fixed amount back per month, plus interest over a fixed period of time.

It makes sense that the quicker you can pay it back, the cheaper it works out, because interest doesn't compound as much. For example, borrow £10,000 with an interest rate of 5 per cent for two years and monthly repayments would be £438 and you would pay £517 in interest. For the same sum borrowed over ten years monthly repayments would be lower, £105, but you would pay £2,663 interest.

Personal loans usually range from between £1,000 and £25,000 over terms of one to seven years. These might be sold as 'home-improvement loans' or 'car loans', but they are the same type of product, just labelled differently. Watch out for fees attached if you repay your loan early, for example, or miss a payment. You might be charged fees for setting the loan up in the first place.

Interest rates on loans and credit cards are advertised with a typical or representative APR. APR stands for the Annual Percentage Rate, and it takes into account not just interest but also any other charges you have to pay, such as arrangement fees, for a loan. The descriptions 'typical' or 'representative' are there because not all borrowers get the advertised APR. In fact, only 51 per cent of applicants have to receive the advertised APR. How much you can borrow and at what interest rate depends on your credit score. Like a mortgage, the best deals are offered to those with the best track record. If yours is shaky you may be one of the 49 per cent that will not get the interest rates advertised, or you may find you cannot borrow as much money.

• TOP TIP

You want to try to borrow the smallest amount possible and pay it off in the shortest term. However, there is a strange quirk of the personal-loan market that means banks charge lower interest rates on larger loans. It may therefore be wise to borrow slightly more than you need, stashing the excess in a savings account. For example, borrow £6,000 as a flexible loan over two years from Lloyds Bank, and you will be charged a rate of 15.5 per cent interest, repaying £165.46 a month, and paying £1,942 in total interest over the four-year term. Borrow £7,500 for four years, however, and the rate drops to 4.6 per cent, which means you will pay £171.05 a month, but interest of £710.19 (assuming you do not clear it earlier), saving £1,231.81. The same is true of Bank of Scotland and TSB, where rates on their personal loans of £7,500 are nearly a third of the rates on £6,000.

This is because more people want to borrow about £7,500, so the market for these mid-priced loans is more competitive, thereby pushing interest rates down. The current average APR on a loan of £7,500 is 4.7 per cent, and on £10,000 and £15,000 it's 4.6 per cent, according to the analyst Moneyfacts. The average APR on a loan of £1,000 is 20.6 per cent, and on £2,000, 19.5 per cent.

Payday loans

The main defence for the existence of payday loans is that if they were banned, desperate people would turn to loan sharks instead, and loan sharks can kneecap you if you don't repay the money you owe them. With this in mind (that a payday lender is only to be used when the alternative is being kneecapped), avoid, avoid, avoid, especially if you want to get a mortgage. Payday loans offered by companies such as Wonga are car-crash expensive if you can't pay them back within days. The clue is in the name: they are there for those who need tiding over until their next pay cheque, or a sudden injection of emergency cash, and allow you to borrow small sums, £50 to £1,000, super-quick, within minutes on your phone in the back of an Uber on a night out for example (not to be recommended), hence the danger.

To borrow, you will be charged a large 'fee' rather than an annual interest rate. The APR equivalent of Wonga's short-term loan product fee would work out as 1,509 per cent, because they are absolutely not designed to be paid back over a long period of time (or you could take the cynical view that they absolutely are, cashing in on people who are not in control of their finances).

Some mortgage lenders will never give a mortgage to someone who has ever taken out a payday loan, even if you have paid back on time. Others take a very dim view if they appear on your credit score, so tread particularly carefully if you are trying to buy a property in the next year. Payday-loan prices are now capped by the government because they are considered so debilitating. As a result you will not have to pay back more than double the amount you borrowed. If you borrowed £50, you cannot be charged more than £100, all fees and interest considered. But that is still a huge amount.

• •

Credit cards

If you get your head around credit cards and how to use them well, they can be extremely cheap and useful, even lucrative if you collect air miles or cashback. They are the best way to borrow small sums of money, in fact, but banks and credit-card companies profit hugely from you tripping up. This is how they make money, offering all sorts of types with different rules and confusing small print.

Do your research, try to pick cards that fit your lifestyle, and be honest with yourself about how much self-discipline you have before rolling out the plastic. **'Extreme optimists have been shown to have preferences for credit card features that are inconsistent with their subsequent borrowing behaviour,' concludes the Financial Conduct Authority.** Too optimistic, and interest can soon get out of hand and you will end up handing over hundreds, even thousands of pounds to banks unnecessarily. A total waste of money that could go towards a house deposit or holiday, instead.

Credit-card basics

When you take out a credit card you are given a credit limit. This is how much you are allowed to spend on it, and it can vary from hundreds to tens of thousands of pounds. What card you get is dependent on how desirable a borrower you are. If your credit score is poor you will not have access to such a large limit, but you can usually push it up after you have a card for a while. Many credit-card companies raise limits automatically, which is not ideal if you struggle with self-restraint.

Like loans, credit cards are advertised with representative APRs, but you will not get what is advertised if you have a less than dazzling credit score. You may be turned down for a credit card altogether. If you think this is a risk for you, be careful before you apply; every application leaves a mark on your credit score. A future lender will not be able to see that you were rejected, but too many applications in a short space of time will damage your score further (see the previous chapter for more on how to improve your credit score).

If you are not sure whether or not you will be accepted, start by carrying out a credit-card 'soft search' using an online tool, which will give you an indication of what kind of APR and credit limit you can expect to receive. All credit cards will set you a time frame in which you can repay your outstanding balance in full without getting charged any interest. For most, this period is a month. Watch out: usually you get charged immediate interest on any cash withdrawal you make on a credit card at an ATM. Never use your credit card for cash withdrawals if you can help it.

If you cannot afford to clear your full balance in a month you need to make the minimum repayment instead. This is a set amount that you must pay or face extra-steep fees, or the loss of perks of the cards like cashback. Credit-card companies LOVE people who only ever make minimum repayments, because it makes them so much money in interest. You have to clear the minimum payment every month, even if you have hardly any debt outstanding. I've seen instances where someone has paid double the minimum repayment one month but skipped the next, thinking they were well covered. Not so: they were still hit with a £12 fee. Set up a direct debit from your bank account to avoid this.

If you only ever clear the minimum repayment you will pay a huge amount of interest over time. See the example I use in the introduction to this chapter – over £7,000 to borrow just £3,000.

Types of credit cards, their pros and cons

• 0 PER CENT PURCHASE CREDIT CARD

PROS If you want to borrow a big lump sum on a card, a bit of extra cash for doing up your kitchen, or towards wedding expenses, for example, then opt for a 0 per cent purchase card. This allows you to borrow interest-free for a set period and only pay off minimum payments without attracting any charges. Periods can be long, twenty-eight months is the most impressive around at the moment, which means that you have just over two years to repay your loan without interest being charged.

CONS You must never miss a minimum monthly repayment or you will lose the 0 per cent deal, which if you have a big balance could be painfully expensive. You need to make sure you do indeed clear the full balance during the interest-free period or you will be hit with an extra-high APR.

• 0 PER CENT BALANCE-TRANSFER CREDIT CARD

PROS The best way to deal with any existing credit-card debts you may have is to shove them onto a 0 per cent balance-transfer card. These cards let you move a 'balance' from elsewhere on which you are paying high interest across to a card where you do not have to pay interest on it at all for a set period. Again this can be long – the longest at the moment lasts thirty-six months. If you are paying interest on a credit-card debt you should do this asap.

CONS As with 0 per cent purchase cards, you must make minimum repayments or face losing the 0 per cent deal. Make sure you do clear it in time, or you will be hit by an extra-high APR after the deal is over.

Balance-transfer cards often come with a fee, usually calculated as a percentage of your outstanding debt, such as 1.99 per cent. That means if you were moving across £2,000 you would have to pay £39.80. This is a lot cheaper than the debt you would pay on an APR of 20 per cent, however, so still worth it. Some balance-transfer cards have no fees, but a shorter 0 per cent period. If you are confident you can pay

down your debt relatively quickly then these are best. Also be careful not to spend on a 0 per cent balance-transfer card. You will be charged high interest rates for doing so.

• 0 PER CENT MONEY-TRANSFER CREDIT CARD

PROS If you need to pay off a debt, or want a cash loan, but you cannot use a credit card to do so – maybe you owe someone money – you can get a money-transfer card. These are also a good way of paying off a high-interest overdraft. They let you transfer cash from the card into your bank account without paying interest for a set period of time.

CONS Get the card provider to transfer the money into your bank. Do not take the cash off the card yourself, or you will pay interest. As above, keep an eye on the 0 per cent deal length and do not bust it, or you will pay eye-watering interest.

• CASHBACK OR AIRLINE MILES CREDIT CARD

PROS If you are confident that you can shop regularly using a credit card and clear the balance in full each month, then getting a cashback card is smart. You will earn rewards every time you spend, and some of those available to people with good credit scores are really generous. If you got the American Express preferred rewards gold credit card, for example, you would receive 20,000 reward points as a welcome bonus, which can be converted into enough air miles to fund a return flight to the Caribbean on Virgin Atlantic (watch out, it is free in the first year but then there is a charge of £140 a year thereafter).

CONS You often have to spend quite a lot of money on your card to pay the cashback points pay, for example, £2,000 in the first three months of owning the American Express card mentioned above, so they are best if you are about to go on a big spending spree, poised to redo your bathroom or buy lots of furniture. There is no point in having a points card if you are not likely to be able to pay off all the balance, because any benefit will be cancelled out in interest charge.

• BAD CREDIT CREDIT CARD

PROS If you have a rubbish credit score you might struggle to get a credit card, but chicken and egg: getting a credit card is one of the best ways to build up your score by showing you can borrow small amounts and pay them back on time. One solution is the credit cards that are marketed specifically at those who have a poor score, for example the Marbles card, or cards by Aqua.

CONS The APRs can be unbelievable, as much as 59.9 per cent, so get this only if you really need to improve your credit score and are supremely confident that you can pay off your balance in full every month.

• •

Overdrafts

Overdrafts do not sound that risky, because those of us who were students got used to relying on them when we were studying, when you could get massive interest-free allowances if you overspent from one month to the next. Do not be lulled into a false sense of security. Once any interest-free period ends they are as expensive, sometimes more so, than payday loans. **If you go into your unauthorized overdraft by just £100 for thirty days, you will be charged more than a payday loan by thirteen of the banks investigated by the consumer group Which? Santander would charge you £179 (on top of the £100), TSB £160, HSBC £150. The**

same payday loan over the same period would cost you £24. The average APR for a £10,000 personal loan is 3.79 per cent, but the average rate for an overdraft is 19.72 per cent, according to figures by the Bank of England.

Overdrafts are either 'authorized' or 'unauthorized'. Your authorized one is the one you sign up for when you open a current account. Lots of banks let you dip into the red by a certain amount, some interest-free, though mostly you have to pay for this facility. If you spend beyond that overdraft, you are into unauthorized territory, which is where you will get stung even harder.

To make matters worse, it is virtually impossible to compare overdraft charges. The money research company Defaqto identified at least thirty different methodologies used by banks to calculate the cost of authorized and unauthorized overdrafts. Some banks charge a set daily fee, others an interest rate, some a monthly fee. The cheapest charging structure for you varies on how frequently you go overdrawn, by how much, and how long you tend to stay in your overdraft. For authorized overdrafts, fees range from 50p to £3, daily, weekly or monthly, and interest of around 15 to 20 per cent. Unauthorized fees can be one-off or monthly charges of as much as £35 or more. Daily fees can go up to £10 a day, or you might be charged a transaction fee of as much as £25 for taking out cash or sending a direct debit when you are in the red.

As a quick rule, banks that charge simple interest rates tend to be cheaper than those that charge a fee or a combination of interest rate and fee. Lots of banks have switched to a fee-based structure because it appears easier for the customer to work out, but this does not mean it is cheaper.

The worst accounts are those that charge a monthly fee, believes Andrew Hagger of the website moneycomms. For example NatWest and TSB both charge a £6 monthly fee for authorized overdrafts, which works out as twenty times more than the under 30p levied by the five other banks who charge a percentage fee, including First Direct, M&S Bank, Metro Bank and Starling.

Banks are fairly happy to lend at high cost, too. The debt charity StepChange says that one client was offered an overdraft of £2,250, though they earned only £200 a month. If you are someone who dips into your overdraft it really pays to work out how much this is costing you, and whether switching to another bank will save you money. Also make sure you are with a bank that has an authorized overdraft buffer, ideally an interest-free one.

It is easier than you may imagine to switch current accounts; see the savings chapter for more information on how. Friends have told me in the past that they could not do this because they were in their overdraft, but actually that does not always matter. If your overdraft is small you might still be able to switch. If not, consider a 0 per cent money-transfer credit card to pay off your overdraft so that you can move somewhere cheaper.

Car finance

In 2017 88 per cent of new car sales were funded using financing agreements. Most of them are not 'bought', however. The majority are actually just borrowing their cars and never own them outright, using deals called personal contract plans – PCPs. These are loans that help reduce the upfront cost of a pricey new car. The amount you borrow is based not on the full price of the car, but on the value of the car once the end of your loan deal is reached, usually after about three years, when the car has depreciated in price.

This is how they work: you pay a deposit, usually about 10 per cent of the current cost of the car you want to buy. You then borrow a sum based on how much the lender predicts the car will depreciate in value over the period of your loan (most deals last two or three years) minus the deposit.

You pay this back monthly, plus APR of about 3 per cent to 10 per cent. At the end of the term you have to give the car back. You could upgrade to borrow another car and take out a new deal, and if the car has not depreciated as much in value as first thought, you might have some 'equity' that you can use with the same dealership to transfer to a new one. Or you can choose to pay a bit more and buy your car. If you choose to buy you stump up for what is known as a 'balloon payment'. The cost of this payment, measured as a 'guaranteed minimum future value' (GMFV), is agreed when you take out the deal. You usually have to pay a bit extra, a few hundred pounds on top, to go for the balloon-payment option.

PCP is a good-value option if you are not sure whether or not you want to own the car, because monthly repayments are relatively low. However, another form of car finance known as car leasing, where there is never a possibility of owning and you just pay to lease the car for a set period of a few years – like extended holiday car hire – is usually cheaper, so do compare. Unfortunately you are less likely to be offered a car-leasing option by pushy salesmen, because dealerships make more commission on PCP.

If you actually want to own your car there are more affordable ways of borrowing to do so, too. Hire purchase, for example, which is where you pay a deposit, about 5 to 10 per cent of the car's value, then fixed monthly instalments over an agreed term, at the end of which you own the car.

The comparison site Go Compare worked out an example to show the difference. Say you wanted a Ford Fiesta with a price tag of £20,270. If you were to approach a Ford showroom you could be offered a Ford Options PCP deal. With a deposit of £1,500 you could 'borrow' the car over thirty-six months, paying £330.99 a month. You could hand it back after thirty-six months and would have taken ownership of it for that period for a total of £11,915.64, or you could decide to pay a balloon payment of £7,306. You would then own the car outright for a total of £20,741.53 – just under £500 more expensive than had you bought the car outright to start with.

If you had just decided to lease it – through, for example Nationwide Vehicle Contracts – you would have had to find a deposit of £1,309.80, and then pay £218.30 a month for the remaining thirty-five months, handing back the car at the end of the period. You would have paid £9,148.30, including a £198 fee, to have owned it for the same period as the PCP, minus balloon-payment deal, for £2,767,34 less. The vast majority of people who take out PCP do not go for the balloon-payment option, so may be paying more to lease their cars than they need to.

If you were to buy the same car on hire purchase with Ford Acquire it would be slightly cheaper than PCP, with a £1,500 deposit, then a £595.52 a month repayment over thirty-six months, resulting in owning the car at the end of the term for £20,582.81. If you bought the car outright, however, using one of the longest-term 0 per cent purchase credit cards on the market – Go Compare uses the example of Sainsbury's thirty-one-month 0 per cent purchase credit card – you could pay the £1,500 deposit up front, repay the card at £605.48 a month, and secure the car for £20,270. You will need a good credit score to get this card.

There are quite a few expensive ways that you can get caught out on any car-finance scheme. The most significant is with mileage. When calculating how much the car will depreciate in value you have to estimate your mileage. If your circumstances change and you suddenly have to drive much longer distances for work, you could end up having to pay out more at the end of your PCP or leasing deal to cover this extra devaluation. If you were to return a car with 40,000 miles on the clock rather than a 30,000 mileage limit, you might pay 10p a mile excess, a further charge of £1,000.

Some leasing deals also include extra costs for servicing, tyres, tax or insurance; you will also have to pay an extra fee for damage or wear and tear above what is seen as reasonable – a bit like when you take back a holiday hire car. Some have small print stating that you have to get your car repaired or serviced with the main dealer, which may work out more expensive and less convenient than your local garage. If you default on your payments on a hire-purchase deal you may have the car repossessed.

You may be offered a deal with 0 per cent interest, or discounted deposit, but be wary: other parts of the deal will probably be inflated in price to make up for it, for example the balloon payment.

Also compare interest rates between dealerships. Ben Smith, the co-founder of Hellocar.co.uk, a marketplace for second-hand cars that has since closed down, told me last year that a sales rep from a high-street bank that has a car-finance division explained there was a 'sell-in rate' for loans, of say 5 per cent. After that point motor dealers are free to set the rates themselves, and receive a chunk back in commission, he says: 'The gentleman at the bank showed me that if you sell finance at 12.5 per cent you can make a £1,000 margin on a car. I am surprised that this practice is still allowed.'

Peer-to-peer loans

You might find it cheaper to get a personal loan from a peer-to-peer lender, rather than a bank or building society, to buy a car up front or to bankroll any other large expense. These new lenders are crowdfunding platforms which cut out the middleman, and the expensive branches, by operating online. They allow individual savers to lend money directly to individual borrowers, with borrowers paying lower interest rates and savers getting higher interest rates. It is not always cheaper, so check; comparison sites now include peer-to-peer loans. Loans may also be more flexible, for example you may be able to choose your repayment term and may not be charged early repayment fees. If you are a saver using a peer-to-peer platform there is a slight risk of losing money but you have got nothing to worry about if you are borrowing. Try Zopa or Ratesetter.

4
How to budget

'Crabs dig holes according to the size of their shells, like the crab, we must behave proportionally to our means,' but never fear, 'even monkeys fall from trees – we all make mistakes and learning to tackle your finances takes practice.' So go the monthly, animal-themed aphorisms in a little book that took hold in 2018, *Kakeibo: the Japanese Art of Saving Money*, all about how to start your journey to a calmer, richer life by budgeting.

I am a massive fan of anything Japanese, not least calming lifestyle trends; I long to be the kind of person who keeps all their grey marl T-shirts Kondo-ed into Muji perspex boxes. And *Kakeibo* has a particularly lovely tradition. Originating from 1904, it was popularized by Hani Motoko, Japan's first female journalist, as a liberating tool for women, giving housewives control over the household budget and therefore financial decisions. It is all about taking a rational, mindful approach to your money.

Nevertheless, *Kakeibo* is pretty obvious. The word translates as household finance ledger. It is a notebook, the latest UK release version of which is interspersed with feel-good Japanese proverbs, in which you write down each day how much you have spent and look back on it to work out where you are going wrong. In my case, too many work lunches of Itsu king prawn gyoza.

Most of us live in a perpetual state of trying to find more money, for a home, wedding, to have children, buy a car, go on holiday, to pay off our credit-card bills, retire or fund a rainy day. There is only really one way of doing this without earning more: drawing up a budget. Without one we are too weak-minded, and (read on for more details of our failures) psychologically programmed to make terrible decisions, to save money, or keep control of what we are spending. Like keeping your socks tidy, it is not rocket science, even if there is a cool Japanese method that makes you more inclined to give it a go.

• •

Drawing up a budget

Start by understanding how much money you actually have, and where it then disappears. You might want to do this in a beautiful notebook. Writing it out by hand, possibly in a Muji gel pen, is thought to make it stick in your head, a more mindful experience. Or there's always a trusty Excel spreadsheet, the back of an envelope or, easiest, on your phone using a budgeting app: Monzo has changed my life, or at least my Itsu situation. I will come on to Monzo, the first bank I have ever loved, and the best budgeting apps to help you divide up your spending and saving quickly and relatively painlessly.

However, I know people who cannot even look at their bank balance towards the end of the month – I used to be one of them. The struggle is real, but, annoyingly, ignoring the problem will not make it go away. As they apparently say in Japan: 'Spilled water does not return to the tray, once it's spent, your money will not come back! Luckily though, every month is the chance to start afresh, and attempt to spill less water . . .'

The *Kakeibo* method

Most budget planners take some spin on the *Kakeibo* method, which goes as follows: write out exactly how much money you have coming in each month, your salary, any existing savings, windfalls or birthday cards of cash. Then detail all unavoidable, fixed expenditure, i.e. stuff that does not vary in price: your rent or mortgage, council tax and bills, cost of commuting, childcare. Take this off your income and work out what you have left to spend on everything else.

Set yourself a savings target: how much you would like to put aside each month. Subtract this number from your spending amount, and then divide the remaining total into weeks. That sum is how much you are allowed to spend per week. Then day by day write down what it is you are spending, jotting down daily totals next to certain categories: food, beer, books, Spotify. At the end of each week and month reflect where you are at with meeting your target and think about what you would change for next month.

That way you are constantly keeping track of your outgoings.

Simple . . . ?

How much should I save (and spend)?

It does not really need stating that how much you want to or indeed can put away is entirely dependent on how much money you actually have, what your commitments and tastes are, and why you are doing it. As one friend said to me, we are all told to save, but why? What am I actually saving for? Good question. We all know of those kinds of people who die with millions in the bank having never bought themselves a new shirt.

Having said that, even if you do not have a specific goal in mind (house, holiday) you should always have some money set aside for unexpected expenses: losing your job, getting ill, the fridge breaking down. It is often these unexpected expenses that force people into high-cost debt that then mounts into an unaffordable, inescapable pile.

I find it helpful to understand some rough average numbers. Some people swear by the 50/20/30 technique: Fifty per cent of your earnings on essentials: housing, bills, food and commuting; 20 per cent on paying down debt or savings; 30 per cent on everything else, but with housing so unaffordable, this might seem unrealistic.

Financial advisers suggest that everyone should save the equivalent of three months' essential outgoings available to hand in an easy-access savings account for 'emergencies'. So if you spend £1,000 a month on rent, food and energy, you should have £3,000 in readily available savings. If you are lucky enough to have more than six months of emergency cash to hand you should make it work harder and earn more interest by locking it in a higher-paying savings account, investment account or pension (more in the following chapters).

Few do, obviously. Research published in early 2018 found over a quarter of all UK households have no emergency savings at all. **StepChange, the debt charity, suggests that households should aim for the slightly less crazy target of £1,000 of savings for emergencies or unexpected changes in circumstances, to avoid getting into debt via payday loans or credit cards.**

I also find it interesting and slightly alarming, to compare my spending with how much other people manage on from week to week.

Each year the ONS releases a family spending report with a breakdown of how the average household divides up its cash. The most recent one suggests the mean average weekly household spend is £554.20 in the financial year ending 2017. This is made up of £79.70 a week on transport, £72.60 on housing and energy, plus an additional £45.80 on mortgage-interest payments and council tax, £58 on food and non-alcoholic drinks, £50.10 on restaurants and hotels, £25.10 on clothes and shoes, £17.20 on phones and internet, £8.20 on alcohol and £73.50 on recreation and culture (this includes holidays).

As you might imagine, this varies loads around the country. In London and the South East average weekly spending is over £600, in the North West it is £437. Renters in London spent an average weekly amount of £189 on rent, more than two and a half times the average amount spent by renters in Wales, Scotland and Northern Ireland.

Remember that one £3.99 tray of prawn gyoza every work day for a year amounts to £1,037.40.

How to make it easier to set money aside

Use cash more and check your direct debits each month

I noticed on my favourite ever holiday – to Japan, funnily enough – that the Japanese are still really wedded to cold hard cash. You still pay with notes and coins on the bus or for your sashimi supper in a restaurant. Maybe this is why they find it easier to be mindful with their money. Cashless, contactless, online shopping and auto-renewal makes it super-easy to pay, super-hard to monitor what's going out of your account – why do you think companies love it so much? Amazon does not even require your CVC (card verification code) number, an usual hurdle that can stop me from making a particularly impulsive purchase simply because I cannot be bothered to track down my debit card.

In fact we find it psychologically more difficult to part with cash, so are less likely to overspend when we have to pay with notes than when we use contactless and do not even pay attention to the transaction price.

Given my own reliance on Apple Pay I shouldn't be surprised by how many readers write to me at *The Times* in despair that they have accidentally been paying literally years afterwards for a mobile phone, or mobile-phone insurance, or magazine subscription auto-renewals that they had long stopped using. **Companies make a fortune out of making it a massive hassle for you to leave their** clutches: 'To cancel your online-only subscription you have to write a letter to us in a fountain pen that can only be sent recorded delivery by a post office 30 minutes from your flat.'

There are apps to help with this, too. Bean or Emma will monitor your direct debits, and will alert you to any unused subscriptions.

Set up lots of pots and pay yourself first

Be frank with yourself. If it is in your account, you are probably going to want to spend it, or you will do so without paying much attention. Next thing you know you are into your overdraft. And a few lots of £20 off a big lump sum on payday will not feel straight away as if it is making much of a dent. You need to rein yourself in, put the bumpers up on your bowling alley, the financial equivalent of clearing your cupboards of crisps so you have to schlep to the shop.

• CASH IN ENVELOPES

The Japanese way is to take out your allocated budget of cash and put it in envelopes at the start of the month: one for food, one for nights out, and so on. Only let yourself spend what is in them, like when I used to be able to go out taking just £15 for a couple of orange Reef, club entrance and a taxi home. RIP 2003. This also has the potential to make you feel really happy when you come across some cash, like the disproportionate pleasure of a tenner in an old coat pocket.

• MULTIPLE DIRECT DEBITS

My way now is to open multiple bank and easy-access savings accounts, different 'pots' into which I deposit different sums via direct debit. My earnings go into one account, and then I put set amounts into others, a tax-bill savings account, a joint household spending current account with my other half, an easy-access saver for my own personal holiday and clothes-splurge saving, and I set the direct debits to come out weekly. It is then easier to see how much is left over and whether or not I can justify another new mascara, and also helps me save substantial sums with minimum effort. Weekly feels more manageable than monthly.

Some suggest you stow small amounts in different pots every day or every other day – £5 here, £10 there, before you know it you have quite a bit of savings. Some suggest £1 on Monday, £2 on Tuesday, £3 on a Wednesday, etc, but I think this is overdoing the banking admin a bit. Though you can set this up automatically through Monzo if you pair it with the app IFTTT. IFTTT let's you save money for every kilometre you run or cycle in Strava. **You might want to also try the 5.2 money diet: set yourself a couple of days a week where you do not spend anything other than budgeted for food or transport, or ask yourself if you could live on 90 per cent of your salary. If yes, try and do it for a few months.**

Set yourself cooling-off periods: you cannot buy something you want, or that's in your online shopping basket, for at least twenty-four hours, or until after you have been to sleep.

• PREPAID CARD

You could also get a prepaid card and, like a pay-as-you-go phone, load it up with your budget for the week or month, and then use it to spend with like you would a debit card, without the risk of overdoing it and slipping into the red. Beware fees on prepaid cards. A card like Pockit charges 99p for cash withdrawals, and a 99p fee each month that you spend less than £500, and you pay 99p up front to open it. The Optimum card costs £5 to open, but has no fees for spending on it. You are charged to use it for cash withdrawals at ATMs though.

Try Monzo, Starling or Revolut

The easiest way to save using the 'pot' method is via one of the new app banks.

Enter my love, Monzo, 'as close to a cult as a bank can be', according to *The Economist*, with its plain English terms and conditions littered with emojis and hot pink debit card, the millennial's black American Express. I get very excited when I see a fellow Monzo customer wielding theirs. So much for the baby-boomer generation being way smarter at managing their money; 53 per cent of Monzo's customers are between twenty and thirty, 28 per cent are aged thirty to forty.

It is one of several start-up 'challenger' banks. See also the equally great Starling and Revolut, so popular that when it launched it had a waiting list and 'golden tickets' you could send your friends to let them jump the queue. You apply on the app, with a photo of your passport, and a short selfie video where you state your name, and a couple of days later a debit card arrives in the post. It offers you real-time alerts every time you use your debit card, categorizing your spending. For example, it recognizes if you used it in Zizzi and adds your bill into the 'eating out' category. Rather than ploughing through the normal itemized current-account list of transactions, you can finally see just how much is going out each month to Tesco Express.

You can also set up 'pots' where you direct your salary into different compartments to stop yourself spending it all. I also like the coin-jar feature where every purchase you make is rounded up to the nearest pound, with the difference sent into your nominated pot. So if you were to buy a coffee for £2.50 you pay £3, 50p of which is automatically saved.

The benefits of open banking

There is a growing number of really useful budgeting apps that likewise help you track spending and save without it feeling too arduous. New rules were introduced in 2018 that mean all banks must now let you share your financial information with other 'third-party' companies, if you give your permission. This is known as 'open banking' and, it is hoped, will make it easier for people to manage their money by comparing their different accounts, credit cards or savings pots side by side. Third-party companies, startups, and other banks will be able to use your data to come up with innovative ways to help you manage them all in one place, or analyse your transactions and recommend products that are better suited to your spending patterns and lifestyle.

Before the introduction of open banking, some banks had said that they would not be liable for any fraud on your account if you had shared your details with third parties. Now as long as the third party is 'authorized', banks cannot use this excuse. It is up to you to share, and check that the third parties you are sharing with are indeed authorized – that is that they are regulated by the Financial Conduct Authority (FCA), which is the 'watchdog' that oversees the financial services industry. There is an online FCA register against which you can check the name of a company if you are unsure. Some legitimate companies are not authorized with the FCA, so you might want to take the risk on them, but be aware that if you are defrauded using them, you cannot easily get your money back from your bank.

There will be two types of services you need to give permission for. The first is account-information services – that's where third parties see your account information from various different banks in one place. They cannot actually do anything to it, just look at it to see how you are spending. The other is payment-initiation services, where you will be able to pay companies from your bank account rather than through Visa or Mastercard.

You will be asked for your consent to access your information when you sign up to a new online service or app. If you feel there is already more than enough data about you floating around online, then you can ignore the new rules and request that third parties cannot view your banking habits. Also, you might want to think twice about signing up to open banking if you are about to apply for a mortgage. It will give banks greater access to your spending data, which if it involves a lot of nights out in Vegas could count against you when applying to borrow.

Genius budgeting apps available now

• CHIP

This is a savings app that uses an algorithm to analyse your current account to work out how much you can save, then automatically moves these savings into a separate account every few days or week, usually about £10 to £25 five times a month – the maximum is £100 five times a month. You get more interest on your savings the more people you recommend to also use the app, up to a maximum of 5 per cent.

• PLUM

Works along the same lines, but your savings are invested through the peer-to-peer lender Ratesetter (see more on peer-to-peer in the savings chapter). You use it through Facebook Messenger.

• MONEYBOX

Does the same, but your money is invested in the stock market instead. You can also round up your spending on any debit or credit card to the nearest pound with the difference invested, so that you save without really noticing. Though convenient, fees may work out quite high investing this way (more on fees in the investment chapter).

• YOLT

Backed by ING, the Dutch bank, Yolt enables you to view your credit card, banking and savings accounts all in one place, making it easier to manage your spending.

• MONEY DASHBOARD

Offers something similar to Yolt, with colourful graphics and tags to categorize and view your outgoings.

• CLEO

Uses artificial intelligence to monitor your spending and will alert you to when bills are due, or you have overspent in a month.

• SPLITWISE

Lets you split bills with friends or flatmates.

• CIRCLE

Useful to send money to friends via text message.

- **PAYM**

Allows you to use your phone to send up to £50 to other Paym users.

- **STOCARD**

Lets you store all your loyalty cards, Nectar, Boots Advantage Card, etc. on your phone.

• •

Know thyself: lessons from behavioural economics

Managing to budget successfully is clearly not just a practical, rational thing, but an emotional one too. No app has yet figured out how to prevent you ignoring your uncertain future for the benefit of some nice new Adidas Ultraboost. Being aware of your own weaknesses and irrational hang-ups is the first step to overcoming them. If you figure out where you are always falling short because of your emotional responses, you can at least try to avoid repeating your mistakes. That is where behavioural economics can offer some insight.

This is an area of thinking that became fashionable in the early 2000s, when the father of behavioural economics, Daniel Kahneman, won the 2002 Nobel Prize for economics for his work with the late Amos Tversky, even though he is actually a psychologist. Behavioural economics is where economics and psychology meet. It is the understanding of why we make the economic choices we do, and how we are not always as rational as we, and traditional economic models, might like to believe. Here are some examples of where we go wrong.

Anchoring

We are susceptible to paying too much just because a high figure is quoted. We gravitate towards middle values and 'anchor' to them when we lack knowledge of what something 'should' be worth.

This is probably why I break out into a cold sweat at the thought of having to haggle or to work out how much to tip someone. In fact, there's a famous example of the tipping system in New York taxis. On the introduction of new credit-card machines, which automatically suggest a 30, 25 or 20 per cent tip, gratuities soared from the former average of between 8 and 10 per cent to 22 per cent. Passengers suddenly considered 20 per cent a bit stingy. Cabbies reportedly made $144 million of additional tips a year. This applies all over the place: when you automatically choose the second-most expensive wine from a menu, because God knows which one is decent and you don't want to look tight; when you put in an offer for a new home that is based on how 'cheeky' you feel you can be even though the high asking price is set by an estate agent.

How much you are prepared to pay is influenced so much more than you might imagine by how prices are 'set' by companies that want to make money out of us, rather than how much something is actually worth to us in terms of what else we would sacrifice for it, or how many days we have to earn enough to pay for it. This is particularly true when we are unsure of the value of something. We don't know anything about wine, or how much a house might sell for in this crazy housing market, which means we are particularly vulnerable to overpaying.

We overvalue sale items

This also works the other way round. We overvalue 'free things', or things on sale, to the detriment of paying a bit more for something that might make us relatively much happier. We buy from TK Maxx just because something has a yellow sticker on it, not really considering whether we actually want another packet of weird teabags, and what other things we might rather pay for, full price, with the money we are using to buy yet more weird teabags. Companies know this, and will tie us into more expensive products off the back of free or discounted trials.

Endowment effect

This also works because we are not very good at cutting losses, we overvalue things we already own. This is the endowment effect. When we have owned something or used something for a period of time, whether that is something as big as a house or as silly as a Netflix subscription, we feel invested in it and value it more than we would had we never owned it. That's why people over-inflate the value of their own home when they sell, and feel aggrieved that the snooty young couple viewing cannot see how much time and attention went into choosing the perfect shade of grey-green to paint the kitchen cupboards; or why you get sucked into paying more for something on eBay than you would have declared it worth before you started bidding. Or even why we do not switch away from a subscription service after a free trial period has come to an end, or we have an irrational desire to stay with the same bank for thirty years.

Loss aversion

This is linked to the endowment effect. We irrationally prefer not losing something, to gaining it. **Multiple studies show we are more upset by losing £100 than we are happy at winning £100, even though the financial difference is the same. We are therefore irrationally risk-averse, which puts us off making more cash by risking loss – in the stock market, for example – or accepting things like pension payouts from our employers, or the taxman, because we have to give up some of our salary in order to do so, even though the gains far outweigh the losses.**

Herd mentality

This is why Instagram influencers are zillionaires and why people queue for hours outside a not-that-great brunch place. If other people value something highly, then we will too, regardless of what it is actually worth to us. We 'self-herd' when we value something highly because we always have done in the past. We buy the same brand of expensive smartphone, every twenty-four months, paying a premium for it, because it was worth it in the past, without necessarily reassessing whether we, and the world, have moved on, and whether it is still worth it in the present, or whether the smartphone brand knows we will buy it anyway and has upped the price.

5
Where
to save

You have drawn up a budget and figured out how much you can set aside, but where to put it? First you need to understand a bit about interest rates.

• •

Interest rates vs inflation

Interest is the reward you get for putting your money in a savings account, the amount a bank pays you, which in theory makes your savings grow. However, interest rates have to be high enough to beat inflation to do this, otherwise you are actually losing money. Inflation is the way in which the stuff we buy, goods and services, rises in price over the years (deflation is where their value falls).

A loaf of bread or tickets to a football match do not cost the same as they did in 1891. If you hold on to a £20 note for forty years it will not buy you as much as it did then.

Inflation is calculated in various ways, but the measures you are most likely to hear about are the Consumer Prices Index (CPI) and the Retail Prices Index (RPI). These are compiled by surveying the rising or falling cost of a basket of different goods and services. RPI and CPI record different things – RPI includes housing costs, for example – and they are calculated differently, so the rates are not the same. Usually CPI is lower and tends to be what is considered the national statistic of inflation.

The Office of National Statistics works out the rate of CPI by surveying 180,000 price quotations a month of about 700 goods and services thought to represent what the population is spending most money on in any given year. The prices are collected in about 140 locations across the UK, online and over the phone, to work out averaging prices and how they have changed, whether they have risen or fallen. This 'basket of goods' offers a particularly satisfying snoop into society's shopping trolley.

When the basket was first introduced in 1947 it included linoleum, replaced by vinyl floor coverings in 1987; condensed milk, a Derby tweed hat, lamp oil, rubber-roller table mangle, soap flakes and cod liver oil. Alcopops were introduced in 1997, along with CD-ROMs, Eurotunnel fares, and a 'casual jacket' in the 'women's outerwear' section. In 2007 credit-card charges and mortgage-arrangement fees were included, while olive oil replaced vegetable oil and recordable DVDs replaced blank VHS cassette tapes. New arrivals in 2018 include exercise leggings, GoPros, chilled mashed potato and body-moisturizing lotion; goods that have come out: a bottle of lager in a nightclub, cash-machine charges and leg waxing.

Inflation rates are recorded in percentages. At the time of writing inflation is 2.3 per cent, which means the things we buy are, on average, 2.3 per cent more expensive than they were last year; and you need 2.3 per cent more money to buy the same things as you bought a year ago.

Whenever you hear the expression 'index-linked' it means that whatever it is rises in step with inflation, usually either RPI or CPI. State pensions are index-linked, for example, as are student-loan repayments and some salaries. When people refer to 'frozen' wages it is because they are no longer pegged to an inflation index and therefore not rising as fast as the cost of what you use your salary for, so you are essentially earning less than you were in previous years.

The government publishes an inflation target for the Bank of England. The Bank also sets the national interest rate, known as the base rate or the Bank Rate. The two are linked: when inflation rises, so the base rate is likely also to rise. Higher interest rates induce people to spend less and save more, which tends to bring inflation down. All this is a long-winded way of explaining that inflation damages cash savings, which makes it even more important to try and protect them with a generous interest rate. Unfortunately, this is difficult at the moment.

In my second-ever article for *The Times* in 2008, in a little feature within the money section called 'savings watch', I wrote slightly apologetically that the best easy-access savings account was offering 6.6 per cent return. At the time of writing this book, the very best interest you can get on an easy-access savings account is 1.3 per cent (about half the rate of inflation), and that is a rarity. Many savings accounts pay less than 0.5 per cent. HSBC pays 0.05% on its flexible saver. Since the credit crunch, interest rates have slumped to historic lows. This has benefited small businesses and homeowners with mortgages, who can borrow with cheaper interest repayments, but it means that saving is far less lucrative, which makes life even more expensive for those who are trying to raise a deposit to get on the housing ladder.

The 'bank rate' or the 'base rate' is set normally eight times a year, and is the rate that influences how high-street banks set their rates for both mortgages and savings accounts. In July 2007 the base rate was at 5.75 per cent. Six months after I wrote my first article at *The Times* the Bank of England had slashed it down to 0.5 per cent, where it remained until 2016, when it fell to 0.25 per cent. It has since risen a bit, but is far off the old days. This has meant that most savers have been losing money in cash savings accounts for several years.

In response, **there is a strong argument for moving away from cash savings towards investing in the stock market, which generally produces a greater, inflation-beating return. This is only really suitable if you are prepared to lock your savings away for at least five to ten years. I explain in the next chapter how to go about investing for this longer term.** For shorter-term savings, cash wins, but you need to give a bit of thought to where to put your cash to minimize by how much it may be eroded.

Here are your options, their pros and cons.

Savings accounts to consider

Current accounts

The chances are you still have the same current account that you set up when you were offered a free railcard to do so as a university fresher. There is nothing wrong with that, but you might be able to make some money from swapping it up occasionally, and with the savings rate so poor some current accounts offer more attractive 'in credit' interest rates for any money that you keep in your bank account. You can also have more than one current account.

Many banks now offer cash incentives for you to move to them – often £100 deposited straight in, not to be sniffed at. You might get more in vouchers too. For example M&S Bank was running a promotion offering a £125 M&S gift card for new customers, First Direct £170 Bose headphones.

If you travel a lot, it is worth hunting down an account with a debit card that does not charge overseas transaction fees. If you are forever falling into your overdraft, however, pick an account that offers the cheapest one. Check out the debt chapter for more on this. Or you might want a bank that has more intuitive apps, such as Monzo or Starling, mentioned in the budgeting chapter.

Many people are put off by the assumption that it is a huge hassle to tell everyone your new account details and switch across your direct debits. Actually you can do this automatically. The Current Account Switching Service guarantees that all payments going into your account, and all those you have going out, will be moved to a new bank account within seven days, so you do not have to go ringing round your gym and your employer to let them know. When you open a new bank account your new bank will close your old one, and everything will come across within a week. Any charges applied to your account because, say, you miss a payment when the process takes place, will be refunded automatically, and any payments that are made to the wrong account are automatically redirected for three years afterwards. Your bank will contact that person or company within this period to tell them about your new account details.

Easy-access savings accounts

PROS These allow you to get hold of your money immediately, some an unlimited amount of times, others may have a cap on how many withdrawals you can make each year, or may dock interest on months when you withdraw, so read the small print.

CONS Usually offer the lowest interest rates. You pay for their flexibility.

Notice accounts

PROS Like easy-access accounts, you can take your money out when you like without penalty, and they usually pay a bit more interest than easy-access savings accounts.

CONS You have to give the bank 'notice' of say thirty or ninety days before it releases your money, so these are not suitable for cash you might need urgently.

Fixed-rate bonds

PROS The best-paying savings accounts for large sums, and the accounts most likely to beat inflation.

CONS To get the reward you have to lock your money away, and you cannot touch it for the period agreed. You can get fixed-rate bonds for various periods – one year to five years usually. The longer you lock away your money the better the rate. Beware though that if you lock your money away for five years you will miss out on any interest-rate rises.

Regular savers

PROS These often have the best interest rates of all savings accounts, but for smaller sums.

CONS Regular savers reward you for drip-feeding in money each month, up to a maximum, with a great return. You need to be organized to take advantage of these though, for example by setting up a regular direct debit from your current account to maximize the account's reward.

ISAs

PROS Normally any interest you earn from your cash savings is taxed at the same rate as your salary is taxed. A cash ISA (short for Individual Savings

Account) is a type of cash savings account that allows you to earn interest tax-free. (You can also save into a stocks and shares ISA, more in the investment chapter.) When interest rates are so low, and savings sums small, taxable interest does not usually amount to much, £2 on interest of £10, for example, but if you are saving a large sum, for a house deposit, for example, it can add up. You can save in easy-access or fixed-rate ISAs.

CONS ISAs have an annual limit on the amount you can save into them, which usually changes each year, but it is generous: £20,000 in the tax year 2018–2019.

Some think cash ISAs are pointless now because the government has recently introduced a personal savings allowance. This is an amount of interest you can earn before you are taxed on it and is £1,000 for basic-rate taxpayers and £500 for higher-rate taxpayers. The advantage of an ISA is that you can build your savings year on year. If you pay into an ISA every year for say twenty years your now, hopefully, large interest will still be tax-free.

Some non-ISA savings accounts pay better interest, so you need to weigh up what is most beneficial to you.

Junior ISA

PROS There are several other types of ISA, designed to help you save for a house deposit or retirement (see accounts for saving for a deposit, below) or for your children. The latter are known as Junior ISAs. These allow you to save tax-free for a child, for their university education for example, and offer generous interest rates.

CONS Whatever money has built up in a Junior ISA becomes instantly available to your child when they turn eighteen, at which point they can withdraw it or continue to save using their own adult ISA allowance. There is nothing you can do to stop them spending it all on Thai fisherman trousers and Red Bull buckets. You can deposit up to a maximum of £4,260 in the 2018–2019 tax year into a Junior ISA.

Innovative finance ISA

This is a new ISA, introduced in 2016, which lets you save through a peer-to-peer lender tax-free. A peer-to-peer lender is a crowdfunder, a company like Zopa, Ratesetter and Funding Circle, which essentially matches you the saver up with someone who needs your money and is prepared to pay interest to borrow it. They cut out the middleman, the bank, in order for you to get a better savings rate (and the borrower a better loan rate).

Technically, saving with a peer-to-peer lender is considered 'investing', so your savings are not totally safe or covered by the Financial Services Compensation Scheme (see below). You choose how long you want to lock your money away for and receive an interest rate accordingly. Peer-to-peer is a new idea, so deemed more risky than conventional saving. Individuals or small businesses are more likely to default on their loans. Most sites mitigate the risks by spreading your savings between lots of different borrowers, the idea being that it is unlikely that all of them will default.

Financial Services Compensation Scheme

Before the financial crisis the idea of a bank collapsing would have been laughable. Now, not so much. The Financial Services Compensation Scheme (FSCS) is there to bail you out if the worst happens. It guarantees up to £85,000 of savings per financial institution, so if – by some miracle – you have more than £85,000 you should spread it between banks and building societies that are not in the same 'group'. For example, Halifax and Lloyds are considered part of the same institution (Halifax is part of Lloyds Banking Group).

Savings terms and conditions to keep in mind

When opening a savings account read the small print, because there are a few ways in which you could get caught out. Most will have a minimum deposit – this might be £1 or could be much higher, such as £1,000. Some will expect you to maintain a minimum balance of savings in order to receive the full advertised interest rate. You will almost always be penalized, for example by losing any interest you have earned, if you withdraw your money before, or more often than you are allowed to.

Most important, watch out for bonus rates. These play on our reluctance to keep switching our savings around. Many of the best interest rates last just one year, at which point they fall to

something absurd, like 0.01 per cent. If you want to earn the most interest, you will probably have to keep monitoring your savings and changing accounts every twelve months or so. Add a note in your Google calendar as to when each bonus period ends.

- -

Savings accounts to help with buying a house

Help to Buy ISA

If you are a first-time buyer saving up to buy a property, or even just contemplating doing so, putting your money into a Help to Buy ISA is a no-brainer as long as you intend to buy a home worth under £250,000, or under £450,000 in London. (Having said that, if you are definitely buying a property, but not for at least a year, a Lifetime ISA, below, is a more lucrative option.) Lifetime ISAs have fees for withdrawal if you do not use the money for buying a home or retirement. Help to Buy ISAs do not.

If you've got at least three months until you exchange on a home, you are turning down at least £400 of free money if you do not open one, £800 if you are buying with another first-time buyer.

The Help to Buy ISA is a regular savings account, where you deposit a maximum of £200 a month, and in return get a decent enough interest rate of between 2 and 2.5 per cent at the moment (interest is tax-free because it is earned within an ISA), and a bonus from the government of up to £50 (25 per cent of your contribution). You can save up to £12,000 in the account, earning £3,000 bonus on top from the government. The minimum government bonus you can use to buy a house is £400, which means you need to have saved at least £1,600 to make the account bonus work for you. You can however deposit £1,200 to open an account, which means you need save only £200 a month for the following two months to receive the 25 per cent (£400) when you buy. You can start an ISA right before you intend to buy, or use it for a longer-term savings account.

You need to be a first-time buyer, but each Help to Buy ISA applies to each individual. If you are

going in on a property with another first-time buyer you can double up and get up to £6,000 towards your deposit. Because you can only save £200 a month it will take four and a half years to earn the maximum bonus.

Help to Buy ISAs are available to new savers until 30 November 2019, but you can keep saving in your accounts after this point, as long as you claim your bonus by 1 December 2030. They are offered by quite a few banks, so look around for the best interest rate. You are allowed only one Help to Buy ISA at any one time, but you can shift your money between different banks if rates change to get the best return. You can withdraw your money whenever, even if you do not buy a house, though if you do not buy you will lose the bonus.

There has been controversy about Help to Buy ISAs because they are sold as a way for first-time buyers to boost their deposit, but actually, so the reports went, the bonus does not go towards your deposit. This is partly but not wholly true, and definitely shouldn't put you off opening one. Unlike when interest appears in your normal ISA, you will not see the bonus until you are ready to complete on your house purchase. To get it, you let your bank know you are closing the ISA. You will receive a letter from them that you give to your solicitor, who uses it to apply for the bonus. You will probably have to pay an extra fee to your solicitor for the admin (about £60).

This all means, however, that you will not have the bonus in time for exchange of contracts, and on exchange of contracts you normally have to put down a 10 per cent deposit for the property. You can often negotiate this down to a 5 per cent deposit, or argue that you have a bonus on its way, so it should not thwart the sale. Solicitors have said that buyers should not worry, and usually it is not a problem. Your bonus will arrive in time for the final sum of money you move across, mainly mortgage, to buy the property.

Make sure that you actually close your Help to Buy ISA, instead of withdrawing cash. There was one case of a first-time buyer withdrawing all the money from his account and sending it directly to his solicitor. When he then went to close the account the balance was £0, which meant he did not qualify for the bonus. Some banks, such as Halifax, require you to go into a branch to close the account.

Lifetime ISA

At the time of writing there are calls to scrap the Lifetime ISA, which can be seen as a complicated product. For now, while it lasts, here's what you need to know about it. **If you are not buying for at least a year, you are better off in the Lifetime ISA (LISA), which is more generous than the Help to Buy ISA. As long as you are sure you are saving for a home because withdrawal penalties are stiff. It offers the same 25 per cent bonus on top of your savings, but you can save more, up to £4,000 a year, and the bonus is added to your account (so you get more interest on top of it), and you can also use the money for your exchange deposit.** If you saved the full £4,000 a year you will get a government top-up of £1,000 a year. You can also add in lump sums, up to £4,000 a year at once, rather than having to limit it to £200 a month. You can use it to buy any property worth up to £450,000 anywhere in the UK. You have to be under forty to open it, however, and you have to wait for twelve months before you can use the money to buy a house.

You can open a Help to Buy ISA and a LISA, but can only put the bonus towards buying a house on one of the accounts.

You can also use the LISA to invest in the stock market. The LISA functions as an alternative to a pension: you can save into it for either a home, or until you are sixty, though you cannot deposit any new money beyond the age of 50. (More on using a LISA as an alternative to a pension in the pensions chapter). The downside is that, unlike the Help to Buy ISA, you cannot withdraw your cash unless you are buying a house, or until you are sixty, though, whichever is sooner, without being penalized by losing interest.

6
How to invest in the stock market

I carried out a straw poll among my friends and family – Do you invest any money in stocks and shares? Almost all of them, both men and women, said 'Ha ha'. Although reluctant to admit it, many did not even really know what stocks and shares are. Freelancers aside, however, it is not true that my friends do not invest. Full-time workers are automatically put into a workplace pension, even if they do not, as most people do not, understand the first thing about it. Most workplace pensions are invested in the stock market, so if you have been auto-enrolled into your pension and have stayed in it, you are already investing. The next chapter has more on pensions and what auto-enrolment is.

When it comes to proactively investing any savings, though, the general attitude is a) don't you have to be rich? b) don't you have to be good at maths? c) don't you have to know what you are doing? d) isn't it all a bit Surrey golf club?

In short no, no, no, except it is still a bit Surrey golf club, which annoys me. Those who feel confident about money, often middle-aged men in cords, are more likely to generate more of it, and pretend that it is really impressive and difficult to do so. In fact unless you want to go full Wolf of Wall Street, generating a bit of a return to help your savings grow more quickly is not that much more taxing than opening a savings account. It is actually pretty dull, and will only take you an hour or two one evening after work.

To the fellow financially unconfident: please do not let thinking you need to know more than you actually do put you off. Also, do not let others over-egg how risky it is. There are many different ways of investing, some much more 'dangerous'. The type you have probably come across, via Hollywood, is the riskiest big swinging dick, Gordon Gekko or *The Big Short*-style hedge funds, and betting against the market. This is a bad idea for a beginner – basically glorified gambling – and is not the kind of investing I'll be addressing in this chapter. Buying and selling shares in individual companies can be fun and interesting if you have time and spare money, but if you are wanting to invest money that you cannot afford to lose in order to reach a particular life goal (comfortable retirement; ability to bring up kids), then best avoided if you are a beginner. See also bitcoin and cryptocurrency: great if you like gambling, probably not somewhere to stash your essential retirement savings.

There are more steady ways to invest money in companies – via investment funds, for example, either by letting someone choose where to put your money for you, tracking a stock-market index (you should know what all this means by the end of this chapter), or by doing a bit more research and picking your own funds – that **if you follow some golden rules make it very unlikely that you will, over the long term, end up down on where you started. In fact, though it feels safer to put savings in a bank, or under your mattress, you are more likely to lose money this way because of inflation coupled with rubbish interest rates.**

I ask Jason Hollands, who is a managing director of wealth manager Tilney, how worried my friends really should be about losing their money by investing rather than keeping it in a bank. He says:

> It is easy to perceive 'risk' as inherently a 'bad thing', but in an investment world it is not, an appropriate degree of risk is really important, as there is a fairly fundamental relationship between risk and reward. This doesn't mean taking high risks will guarantee high rewards of course – if that were the case it wouldn't be risky – but the potential range of outcomes

widens the more risk you take, and if you are not prepared to accept any risk, then the rewards will be incredibly low. So often the bigger problem is investors not taking enough risk and being too cautious, rather than the other way round.

In order to invest safely you need to be prepared to lock money away for the long term, ideally for as long as you can, but at the basic minimum five years, ideally ten years and beyond. If you are already struggling to afford the cost of living with an income diminished by student-loan repayments and a frozen wage, you may not have much money left over to lock away. Also before you lock away any money you should make sure you have some emergency cash savings available at hand in an easy-access account.

But if you can find a bit of spare cash, or you have a sum as a gift or inheritance that you want to grow, then you should give it a go. Investing in the stock market is great for those who want to save for a pension, or for those who want to save for children or for a future midlife goal, maybe a home deposit if you do not intend to buy for another decade or there is no chance you will get on the ladder until your forties.

Just as there is no right time to start a family, there is no right time to start investing, but with the latter decision at least, the younger you are the better. You have longer to ride out the ups and downs of the market, and benefit from the magic of compounding returns. Here's an example of compounding: you invest £1,000 in year one and earn a 5 per cent return on it. That means that in year two your pot, on which you earn 5 per cent a year, has grown to £1,050. So in year two you are paid 5 per cent not on £1,000 but on £1,050, giving you a higher sum again, £1,102.50 by year three, and so on and so forth over the decades. Even if in some years you get a lower return than 5 per cent, it is still on a much bigger pot than you began with, hence why the longer you can leave it, the better off you will be. In 20 years your £1,000 is £2,653.30.

The investment company Nutmeg illustrates this well. **Taking UK stock-market data between 1970 and 2017, if you had invested in it for just one day at any point since then you would have had a 53.5 per cent chance of making any gains on your investment – about the same as tossing a coin. Invest for one month, and that rises to 62.8 per cent; for one year, 77.8 per cent; for the**

recommended ten years, 98.6 per cent. Someone who invested in the stock market for more than 11.1 years at any point in time during this period would not lose money. If you are willing to leave it for longer, you can afford to invest in much more risky assets, too, which may produce a better return.

Here's an example, from investment platform AJ Bell. If you were to save £500 in a cash ISA with a 1 per cent interest rate, it would be worth £744 after forty years. If you were to put the same in a stocks and shares ISA, earning 4 per cent return after any investment charges (this is a very cautious figure, many investments earn much more, double or triple), it would be worth £2,400. If you assume that inflation was to run at 3 per cent a year, your £500 would actually drop to £223 in a cash ISA, less than half the amount originally invested, while your investment has still grown in real terms to £744.

It is hard to define an 'average' investment return the way you would an average cash-savings interest rate, but, over the last twenty-five years the FTSE All Share (an index of companies you might want to invest in – I will explain) has produced total returns of 9.48 per cent per year. There's no guarantee the next twenty-five years will be as good, but they could also be better. Many experts tend to use 4 per cent or 5 per cent as a fairly conservative estimate of returns for a long-term investor who takes a reasonable amount of risk, but it's all dependent on the risk you take and the performance of the stocks or fund managers you back, which will vary from person to person.

I will talk you through how to get started later in this chapter, but first, a lesson in some investment jargon. You need to understand what the different 'assets' are in order to invest in them.

What are assets?

Assets include cash and property. You are 'investing' by buying a flat that you hope will rise in price so that you get more out of it when you sell than you put in when you bought.

You may also invest in commercial property – that is offices or shopping centres – via funds, or stocks, shares or equity (for the purposes of this book, basically all the same thing), bonds and commodities.

The most successful investors like to have a mixed 'portfolio'. I visualize this as some kind of Nineties Filofax, but it is not a physical thing, rather a collection of investments made up of a mixture of assets, so, as the cliché goes, that your eggs are not all in one basket. If house prices fall, or bank interest rates are crappy, at least you have your shares to fall back on for a comfortable retirement.

Need to know: what are stocks and shares?

Like humans, companies need cash to start up, grow, survive and make a success of themselves in this globalized capitalist world that we live in. Take the very delicious nut-butter brand Pip & Nut, available at a Sainsbury's near you, and thought up by my university flatmate's sister, the lovely Pip. Pip had her smart but simple idea of creating a company that would make and sell healthy nut butters while she was training for the London marathon. Her post-run snack was peanut butter on toast, and she saw a gap in the market for one that was not full of refined sugar and palm oil.

But you can't start a company with absolutely nothing. She somehow needed to find money, or 'capital', to pay for almonds and coconut oil and salt, people and machines to mash them up together, jars to put the mashed-up almonds in, designers to create the jar label, her time to email Sainsbury's to negotiate when they would start stocking her new nut butter, and so on. Where to get it from? One option is to sell little bits of your new company, literally 'shares' in it, with the promise that if it does well the company will be worth more money, and those that own it will be able to sell their share for more than they paid for it. Shares are also known as equity: you own a share, you have an equity stake in a company.

The people who buy these shares, shareholders (or members), benefit just as Pip does if her idea succeeds, everyone loves and buys the nut butter, and it starts to make a profit so that they can sell the shares for more than the price they bought them at. Sometimes a company goes stratospheric and becomes worth a fortune, making whoever invented it, and the shareholders, very smug and rich. Think Zuckerberg and all those mates who owned a little bit of his Facebook idea when, back in 2004, he allegedly described the Harvard students who posted all their personal information and photos of nights out at the union on his new little website as 'Dumb f***s'.

A company can issue only one share, or hundreds of millions. Apple has over 5 billion.

Need to know: what is the stock market?

A company is either private or public. A private company, such as Pip & Nut, or indeed Facebook when it first started out, may issue shares to their family or friends (my old flatmate's got a stake), employees, or professional investors, such as for example 'angel investors' or venture capitalists. These are called 'unquoted' shares, or private equity.

Any old member of the public who wants to benefit from the expected success of Pip & Nut cannot automatically do so by buying shares, unless it 'goes public' and becomes a public limited company (PLC). Companies generally decide to do this to raise more money from lots of investors, which is what Facebook did. Companies have to be of a certain size before they can go public. Once a company has gone public, anyone can buy shares in it, as long as there are shares available. Companies put out a set amount and then, if they wish, sell them on (hopefully for a higher price, making a profit).

This buying and selling is done through the stock market, which is composed of stock exchanges, (stock is pretty much the same thing as shares) on which these shares are 'quoted'. Stock exchanges are places where traditionally people gathered to trade quoted shares, though these days it is usually done online through specialist platforms or share supermarkets (more on this shortly). The London Stock Exchange in the City is one of the world's oldest. The New York Stock Exchange, on Wall Street, and the NASDAQ in the US are the world's biggest.

Need to know: different types of shares

There is a huge variety of different companies from all over the world whose shares are traded on the London Stock Exchange, from little local British ones valued at under £1 million to massive international conglomerates, valued at more than £90 billion. The stock-market value of any company is based on how much its shares are worth in total at any particular moment in time.

The value of each share (and therefore business) rises and falls depending on how many people want in on a particular company, and how many shares are available to buy – it's basic supply and demand. That's why you hear in the news that share prices have tanked after a company has done something wrong and looks less likely to make a profit. For example, the price of shares in the electric-car company Tesla fell after its billionaire owner, Elon Musk, put out a misguided April Fool's tweet saying that Tesla had gone bankrupt. Oops.

If a company has 100 shares, and each is worth £1, or 100p (which is how a share's value is expressed), the company's value, or capitalization, known as 'market cap', would be £100. The biggest companies on the stock exchange are known as large caps, the smallest, small caps, in between, mid caps. Shares for the large-cap companies can be called blue-chip shares.

Shares may be divided into different categories, 'defensive' or 'cyclical', 'growth-' or 'income-'producing. These are based on the characteristics of certain kinds of company, what product or service it is offering, and whether it is more or less likely to be popular at certain times.

Defensive shares are shares in companies that do well even when the economy does not, things that people always need, no matter how much money they have – companies that produce pharmaceuticals, or food, or energy. Cyclical shares do better or worse depending on how well the economy is doing. Think banks (which suffered loads during the recession when people started withdrawing their savings, or could not pay their mortgages) or clothes companies (fewer people buy a new outfit when they are worried about their job situation, but will have a splurge when they get a bonus at work).

Income stocks may refer to shares in long-standing familiar companies. Like a spouse, these companies are usually more stable and reliable. They have been around for ages and you are familiar with what they do, they have established customers and suppliers, so you can take a decent bet that they will stick around for a while longer yet and continue to offer you a steady return on your investment – think BT, or Shell.

As well as benefiting from any rise in value of such companies, investors also get a regular return on income stocks through what is known as 'dividends'. These are a regular payment of a cut of the company's profits handed out to shareholders, a bit like interest on a bank account. You can take these dividend payments out as cash and spend them, or reinvest dividends to benefit even further from compounding.

Newer companies, like someone you're on a second date with, have all the potential to be much more exciting than another night in front of Netflix, but more unstable, less tried and tested. These may offer 'growth' stocks. They also usually pay dividends, but 'yields' or returns on dividends tend to be smaller. Return comes more from capital growth. Amazon and ASOS are good examples.

Need to know: stock-market indexes

To make a judgement on how different types of shares are doing and how the overall stock market is performing, which is a good indication of the health of business and therefore the economy in a country, you need some kind of measure. Step up 'indexes', or 'indices'. There are tonnes of indices, which monitor different sectors – an index to look at the performance of shares in technology companies, energy or property companies, for example. There are also indexes which reflect the health of different countries, based on how their respective businesses are performing.

In the UK the Financial Times Stock Exchange 100 (FTSE 100), for example, comprises the 100 largest companies listed on the London Stock Exchange. The index rises and falls according to the share-price performance of the 100 companies listed on it. It is assessed every three months, and if companies' shares have underperformed they may fall out of the index and be replaced by another. Two or three drop out of the FTSE 100 every quarter. Companies currently in the FTSE 100 include Sky, Burberry, easyJet, ITV, Next, GlaxoSmithKline, Taylor Wimpey and Royal Mail. The index is updated constantly during the working or 'trading' day, and at 4.30 pm a closing price is announced.

There is also a FTSE 250 – the 250 largest companies after the FTSE 100 (Cineworld, Greggs, Games Workshop, Wetherspoon, JD Sports, Ted

Baker, WH Smith), and the FTSE All Share of about 600 companies.

Other famous stock-market indexes, which tell you a lot about the health of a country's economy: the Dow Jones industrial average (or just 'the Dow'), comprised of the thirty largest publicly owned companies in the US (currently including Apple, the Walt Disney Company, McDonald's, Visa, Goldman Sachs), and the Standard & Poor's 500 (S&P 500), tracking the performance of 500 companies with market capitalizations (the overall value of the shares) of at least $6.1 billion (all of the above, plus others like Amazon, Nike, Twenty First Century Fox, Estee Lauder, Gap, Google, Starbucks, Tiffany & Co).

Japan's main index is known as the Nikkei 225. Germany's is the DAX.

Need to know: what are bonds, gilts, commodities?

Shares are not the only thing traded on the stock exchange. Let's say that someone needs cash to start or grow a business but they have no interest in selling any share in it. What is the other obvious way to get money? By asking to borrow some, and then writing out an IOU to whoever says they are happy to stump up a loan for a bit. This is what a bond is.

A small company like Pip & Nut might go to the bank for a loan. For some mega-companies, a bank loan is expensive or restrictive, so they issue bonds, a load of IOUs, in return for big loans from lots of people. When you 'buy' or invest in a bond, really you are just agreeing to lend a company some money. A bank will not offer you a credit card for nothing, so bond investors are not going to loan a company money without compensation in the form of interest payments. Interest payments on bonds are called yields or coupons (in ye olden days bondholders would redeem literal coupons for their interest payments). And just as when you repay your credit card, the loan money is paid back by the company that issued the bond after a certain agreed period, known as the maturity date.

It is not just big companies that issue bonds, but governments, too, who need money to grow their countries, to build roads, railways, schools, armies. UK government-issued bonds are known as gilts, US government-issued bonds are treasuries.

Bonds are also known as 'fixed-income securities', because when you buy one (or lend to a company) you know exactly how much money you are going to get in return for it on maturity: the interest payment or 'yield' is laid out at the beginning of the agreement. If you buy a bond with a value of £100, a yield of 5 per cent, and a maturity of ten years, you will receive £5 a year for the next ten years, a total of £50, on top of your £100 that you'll get back at the end of it.

Bonds are considered less risky than shares because you know how much money you will make from the start, unless a company goes under. And if a company does go under, it is obliged to pay out what is left of it to bondholders before shareholders. Government bonds are generally thought of as even safer, because governments are much less likely to go bankrupt – though not always: see Greece in 2015.

Bonds can be bought and sold on, just like shares, though individual investors do not often buy individual corporate bonds, you are more likely to invest in bonds through a bond fund.

Another asset class to look out for is commodities. These are goods, usually raw materials, that are interchangeable and do not vary a great deal no matter who has produced them. Oil, coal, coffee, gold and silver, beef, wheat and the almonds or peanuts used to make Pip's nut butter are all commodities. These are also bought and sold, and their prices rise and fall depending on lots of different factors such as demand from businesses, which rely on commodities to function (no Starbucks without coffee beans), or how the weather affects them. A drought or unseasonable cold snap in California will hit almond crops, fewer can be grown, the price of almonds soars, this will hit the profits of a company that relies on affordable almonds, like Pip & Nut (and therefore the price of shares in the company, too).

Need to know: what are investment funds?

You could put all your savings towards buying many shares in one company, but think about how risky this is. You like the idea of owning a bit of Topshop – you've been buying Motto jeans since you were sixteen, seems a good bet, so everything you've got set aside for the future goes into buying that slice. But suppose that there's a sudden combination of changing minimum-wage laws in China, so that workers have to be paid more, and heavy snowfall damaging cotton crops, which makes cotton much more expensive. Then a social media campaign calls for a boycott of businesses owned by Sir Philip Green. Plus more people prefer to shop in H&M, whose inventive high-fashion knock-offs are getting way more exposure in the *Guardian* this year. Maybe Topshop can't make money any more. It goes bankrupt. Your share in the company is worth £0, your savings have disappeared. Or, more likely, Topshop is having a bad year just as you want to withdraw all your shares, and they are worth less than what you paid for them. You have lost money.

To avoid this, you need to buy shares in lots of different companies. If you had split your ownership between Topshop and H&M, at least you would have made a bit of money to offset the loss. Better still to own a company that is completely different to Topshop, because H&M could still suffer from changing Chinese wage laws, or the rising price of cotton.

Perhaps you want to some safe corporate bonds too, so you know exactly how much yield you are going to get over the next few years to offset any uncertainty surrounding the performance of your shares. This process is known as 'diversifying' and is absolutely key to investing safely and profitably.

Investment funds help you to diversify. They are a pot in which lots of individual investors can pool their money, handing it over to a fund manager who then decides where to invest their cash for maximum return with minimum risk. They will pick a mixture of shares (remember there are different types of shares too, income and growth, defensive or cyclical, some more volatile than others), bonds or commodities. A fund might also invest in cash and property. Some funds do not have what is known as an 'active' manager but peg themselves to a stock-market index like the FTSE 100, which is also a collection of companies – more on this below.

The choice of what individual shares or bonds to invest in is taken away from the investor in a fund. Instead the individual investor makes a decision about what kind of investment fund they want to put their money into, and the investor receives a proportion of the money that the fund holds. There are different ways of making money out of funds, but I will not go into that here.

There are thousands of different investment funds available, specializing in all sorts of areas and aimed at different types of investor: those who are prepared to take loads of risk with their money, those who want something very safe, and anywhere in between. These funds might invest just in shares in UK companies, for example, or a fund might hold global stocks; they might focus investments in a specific country, say USA or Japan, or in what are called 'emerging markets' such as Brazil and India, just defensive shares, or just income shares. You might have a fund where you invest solely in companies in the technology sector. Other funds might be called things like a fixed-interest fund that invests only in corporate bonds.

You can hold as many funds as you want within your 'portfolio', you can buy a ready-made portfolio made up of a mixture of funds to suit your appetite for risk, or get more involved and pick a spread of funds yourself. Your workplace pension will be invested in funds that your employer's pension provider has chosen, but you can change it, in fact it is a good idea to do so. See next chapter for more.

How to start investing

Start by thinking about why you are investing and what for – your investment and life 'goals' in financial adviserspeak. Your retirement? A house deposit? Your child's future? Or simply to have a bit more money to live on when you reach midlife? This will help inform your decisions about how much risk you are willing to take with your savings and when you will need to withdraw your money or 'cash in' your investment.

The thing to remember is that you want to invest for as long as you possibly can. The longer you invest for, the more money you are likely to make. As I have mentioned above, you should not invest for less than five years any money you definitely want to get back. If you are willing to leave it for longer you can afford to invest in much more risky assets, too, like growth shares, which may produce a better return.

The fortunes of the stock market go up and down, plunging during the financial crisis, for example, when shares were worth much less than many people had paid for them. For investors this was alarming. They had, on screen, lost a

huge amount of money. But for those who had been investing for years previously, and have left their money in since, it did not matter so much: the high points over decades make up for the low points, and those who remained invested in the market would have seen their money recover by now. That's why the advice is so often, for the amateur investor, or even the very professional, to choose where you want to put your money and leave it there. If you have a nervous disposition, try not to look at it too often, because you might get cold feet, though do check it about once a year to see if you are on track to meet your goals, and to readjust if not. Do not panic if markets fall and respond by taking out all your investments just as their value hit its lowest point.

Trying to 'time' the market is often considered a mistake, because you end up investing when things look good and the market is riding high, subsequently shares are pricey, and then take your money out when everything is crashing, just as shares are at their cheapest. If a company is doing very well and everyone is excited about it, the chances are that rush has already been priced into its shares.

Warren Buffett, the world's most successful stock-market investor, writes regular letters to shareholders in his company. In one he wrote:

> During the extraordinary financial panic that occurred late in 2008, I never gave a thought to selling my farm or New York real estate, even though a severe recession was clearly brewing. And if I had owned 100 per cent of a solid business with good long-term prospects, it would have been foolish for me to even consider dumping it. So why would I have sold my stocks that were small participations in wonderful businesses? True, any one of them might eventually disappoint, but as a group they were certain to do well. Could anyone really believe the earth was going to swallow up the incredible productive assets and unlimited human ingenuity existing in America?

How much can you invest?

It is a myth that you have to be rolling in it to invest, though if you are in (non-student-loan) debt, feeling cash-strapped, and do not have any rainy-day savings in an easy-access savings account, it is probably not for you.

Many companies have minimum contributions of £50 a month, but some, such as Wealthify, an online investment platform, let you start with as little as £1. Others let you start with an initial sum of from £500 to £1,000. Much advice suggests that instead of investing a big amount of cash you invest a regular small amount, maybe monthly, so that you are not tempted to 'time' the market. If the stock market goes down you simply buy at a cheaper price the following month – it should even out. If you were to save £50 a month for your child when it is born then you could have a lump sum of about £17,400 by the time the child is eighteen if markets behave as they have done in the past, with 5 per cent average growth a year.

Need to know: investment fees

Unlike most savings accounts, when you are putting your money into an investment fund, or buying shares directly, you have to pay fees for your investments to be looked after. It is important to consider when choosing where to invest how much you want to pay in fees, because they will erode your savings quite substantially if they are high.

These fees include an investment-management charge, which is deducted from the value of your investment to pay for the costs of selecting investments for the fund, and various admin fees. These range from 0.75 per cent of the value of your fund up to 1.25 per cent or more, and you pay the fees as an annual charge.

You will most likely invest into your fund or funds, or even buy individual shares if you're feeling bold, through a 'platform', or fund supermarket. These companies will administer your investments and let you manage your portfolio online, offering useful tools, advice and graphics to show how your portfolio is doing, what kind of investment options you have and so on. To use them you have to pay a fee, too, usually about 0.45 per cent of the cost of your investments a year.

Active vs passive investment

Some funds are more expensive than others because they are 'actively managed'. That is they are run by a person, known as a fund manager (many of whom are considered 'star managers' and have celebrity-like status among money nerds), who actively pick what a fund should invest in. These managers and their team do loads of research into different companies using their expertise and often long track record of making profitable decisions to pick the best selection of assets.

They produce loads of information and statistics that you as an investor can pore over to decide whether you rate their expertise above another star fund manager's expertise. Remember though that someone picking the right stocks last year does not guarantee that they will do so in the coming years. Arguably they are reading a crystal ball, guessing what is going to happen to the economy, the weather, consumer appetite for different goods and services, which businesses look like they will survive well into the future, which look overvalued or undervalued, and so on.

There are many who think, therefore, that active management is a waste of money, that you cannot 'beat the market', and the only fund you need is a tracker fund: one that is passive, and simply 'tracks' one of the indexes I mention above. You might invest in a fund that tracks the FTSE 100, for example, its value (and therefore the value of your money) rising and falling with the value of the UK's

100 most valuable businesses. Or one that tracks the US S&P 500, rising as US business booms, falling when the US stock market looks a bit ropey. Over time these peaks and troughs should even out, because, as Buffett says, there is unlimited business ingenuity and profitable assets out there. Hopefully.

Because no one is having to do any research, tracker funds are cheaper to invest in. Whether you prefer the active or the passive approach is something you have to decide. You could of course opt for a bit of both.

What platforms to consider

When choosing the platform through which you can invest in funds (or individual shares, though as I said, that is not advisable for beginners), you need to consider the total size of your investment pot, and how often you will be buying or selling shares or funds. Some platforms charge for trading, and how much support you need to do so. They vary a lot, from platforms that just present you with thousands of investments to pick, to others that offer online tools and investment information to help you make choices.

There are three main types: do-it-yourself platforms that offer the biggest choice and are set up for confident investors who want to make all investment decisions themselves; the 'do it with you' platforms with more information and tools, and suggested lists of best-buy investments; and a range of investment funds by risk profile, for those who do not have the time or confidence to choose all their investment themselves. Be aware, however, says Steven Nelson, head of research for the financial research company the Lang Cat, that many of these ranges are managed by an in-house fund manager, so in some respects you're being sold to as much as you are being helped. The final decision on the portfolio remains down to the investor.

'Do it for you' platforms, which are sometimes called robo-advisers, have ready-made investment portfolios that take away any responsibility for the investment decision. Beginners may feel happiest opting for a platform with these ready-made investment portfolios, and a simple charging structure.

Justin Modray, of Candid Financial Advice, says that for smaller sums, platforms that charge an annual percentage fee with no hidden extras such as fund-dealing fees are a good place to start. They can be more expensive if you have tens of thousands of pounds invested. The tipping point for opting for a flat-fee provider is usually about £100,000, but I imagine that is unlikely to be an issue for you for some time.

Most suggested portfolios will contain about half a dozen funds, and you can choose one depending on whether you want low, medium or high risk (again, you can afford to take more risk if you intend to leave your investment intact for a long time).

Choosing one of these reduces the chance that you will make a bad or inappropriate choice of where to invest. If you want to pick yourself, Modray recommends considering a low-cost index-tracking fund, maybe combined with one or two actively managed funds. Try to ensure a spread across global stock markets and investments like bonds and property that are unlikely to all move in the same direction at the same time. **Modray recommends fund platforms Cavendish Online and Close Brothers, which both charge 0.25 per cent, so that if you had £10,000 invested you would pay £25 a year. Fidelity charges 0.35 per cent (£35); Hargreaves Lansdown 0.45 per cent (£45).**

Richard Bradley, head of data for website Boring Money, suggests Nutmeg, an easy-to-use robo-adviser, where you can answer a simple questionnaire to be guided into a set of investments that suits you best. Also Aviva, 'a safe, mainstream choice, here you can pick between four ready-made investment portfolios'; Wealthify, good for those who like a well-designed simple service, works well on a mobile, with five choices; and Charles Stanley as 'one for beginners who want to learn more and slowly spread their wings', with both simple starting options and a full range of further choice should you move on to that.

You should consider tax when investing. Though your returns will probably not be huge when starting out, you are taxed on any income made through dividends and the growth in value of your investments. You get a tax-free allowance for this (see more in tax chapter 8), but it is wise to start investing through a stocks and shares ISA, where all of your returns are tax-free. You could also consider a Lifetime ISA if your goal is to invest for a house deposit (see savings chapter for more on the LISA) or retirement. For more on how to invest tax-efficiently in your pension, turn to the next chapter.

7

Everything you need to know about pensions

Pensions are probably the least sexy of all very unsexy personal finance topics. Saving up for a distant point in an unpredictable future (what if I'm hit by a bus tomorrow after living an unnecessarily crap, frugal existence?) into an account that you can't touch for decades is the worst kind of saving. At least putting aside money for a flat deposit or travelling, even a new washing machine, gives you something tangible to value and anticipate.

Saving for an unknown future becomes even harder when there are many more immediately pressing commitments for which you need to find often non-existent extra cash. When middle-aged wealthy pension bods bore on about the insane amount of savings you need to find to fund your retirement, it is tempting to feel affronted and switch off completely. Nevertheless, it's so worth while to engage with how pensions work while you are young – mainly just so that you can decide whether you want to put a plan in place and then forget about it. Having youth on your side will make it much easier to save more by giving up less money each month, thanks to the magic of time, and compound interest.

Here are the basics to get you started.

So what is a pension?

The aim is to have some money to live on when you are old so that you do not have to work until you drop dead, especially bearing in mind that **a 25-year-old woman's average life expectancy is now ninety-one, and she has a 19 per cent chance of reaching one hundred,** at which point she probably does not want to be still selling screws in B&Q.

The government are keen to encourage people to save up for their eighties and nineties while they are young and earning money, given the vast expense of supporting a (massively growing) generation of older people who may not be well enough to earn. You will start receiving benefits in the form of the 'state pension' when it deems you of retirement age – an age that it sets, and which is creeping ever upwards.

State pensions are paid out of a compulsory tax you pay throughout your working life, known as National Insurance. If you do not pay enough National Insurance you do not get the state pension. Note, however, that this National Insurance does not go into an account that is left untouched until your retirement; it is added to the government coffers each year, like all other tax that you pay. That is why people refer to the state pension as a Ponzi scheme, which is where whoever owns the scheme generates returns for established investors through money paid by new investors. Your National Insurance is currently funding today's retirees' state pensions. If the government of 2050 decides to abolish state pensions just as I retire I will not be able to claim a refund on all that National Insurance I've already paid.

The government also encourages you to save for retirement before you stop working, through super-generous tax breaks to enable you to accumulate a 'private' pension.

At its most simple therefore, a private pension is really just a tax break, or what is known as a tax 'wrapper' – a bit of jargon meaning something you wrap around a variety of different products to protect it from tax. The product is most commonly an investment fund, where your money (hopefully) grows by investing it in the stock market, but you can hold other things in a pension, like cash, or commercial property.

There are zillions of different pension products and funds with grim undecipherable names and fees and percentages attached, part of the reason the area is a headache to understand, but that should not put you off taking advantage of the basic tax break, which is as close as you can get to free money. The downside to the generous tax break: you have to lock away your money in an account that you are not allowed to touch until you are fifty-five. That's why a pension is a more lucrative way to save for retirement than an ordinary savings account or wodge of £50s under a mattress. You do not pay as much tax on it as you would if you were just bunging some extra money into your current account and ignoring it until you reached your seventies.

The state pension

As it stands, anyone retiring today receives a 'full' state pension of £164.35 a week (true to tax year 2018/19), that is £8,546.20 a year, provided they have accrued at least thirty-five years of National Insurance contributions. You need at least ten years of National Insurance contributions to get any state pension at all; you get an accordingly reduced amount if you have between ten and thirty-five years.

You pay these National Insurance contributions automatically if you earn more than £162 a week (in 2018/19). If there are periods of your life where you do not work, because you are on maternity or paternity leave, say, or bringing up children, are unemployed, caring for someone else, or too unwell to earn, you could struggle to make up thirty-five years' worth. You can resolve this by claiming National Insurance credits. Some are paid automatically – for example if you are on statutory maternity pay or claiming child benefit – or you can plug the gap by making voluntary contributions. You can request your National Insurance record at any time to see if you are on track to meet the thirty-five-year requirement.

At the moment the state pension rises year on year, by a minimum of either 2.5 per cent, the rate of inflation (CPI, short for consumer price index, see chapter on saving for more explanation of what that is), or by the average earnings growth, whichever is greater. This generous guarantee is what is called the 'triple lock', introduced in 2011 by the coalition government. It is controversial for its generosity, rising much more quickly in recent years than earnings and the prices of stuff you might want to buy, meaning pensioners have seen their incomes grow relatively much faster than people in work. As a result the triple lock is not expected to last beyond 2020. There is talk of downgrading it to a 'double lock', removing the 2.5 per cent guarantee. What the state pension will look like by the time those in their early thirties reach their sixties in the 2050s, however, is anyone's guess.

You might be taken aback to learn just how expensive pension benefits are as we all live longer. In the financial year ending 2017, the UK government spent £264 billion on welfare, which made up 34 per cent of all government spending. Of this welfare budget, £2 billion – that is 1 per cent – was spent on unemployment benefit, £111 billion – 42 per cent – was spent on pensions.

The age at which you receive your state pension is rising to try to reduce the cost of this massive bill. As of November 2018 it is sixty-five for both men and women, up from sixty for women a few years ago. From 2019 it will rise for men and women to reach sixty-six by October 2020 and sixty-seven by 2028.

Young people will probably not get it before at least seventy though, according to a report commissioned by the government that recommended that anyone born after 1987 should wait until they are seventy for the state pension.

Private pensions

All this demonstrates that an income of just over £8,500 a year (or whatever the equivalent sum will look like in forty years' time after inflation) is probably as good as it's ever going to get. That will not buy you many Galapagos cruises. You are going to need to save more.

• WORKPLACE PENSIONS

The recent introduction of what is known as 'auto-enrolment', another way the government is trying to nudge us into accruing enough, means every employer must help all of its employees over the age of twenty-two and earning at least £10,000 to save into a private pension by placing them into a workplace pension scheme.

The law sets minimum contributions each year, that is the amount that is annually paid into the pension scheme, a giant pot of money that you and your colleagues will be able to dip into when you all turn fifty-five. This is rising. At the moment it is 5 per cent of anything you earn over £5,876 and up to £45,000. So if you earn £25,000, at least £956.20 will go automatically into a pension for you (£25,000–£5,876 = £19,124, 5 per cent of £19,124 is £956.20).

Note that the 5 per cent, or £956.20, is not all going to come out of your £25,000 earnings. That contribution is made up of three chunks of money:

1 Money that you pay out of your pre-tax salary (a minimum of 2.4 per cent at the moment). Generally this comes out before you receive it, so you will never see it, you will just get less money put into your bank account on payday.

2 Money that you are paid by your employer on top of your salary (at least 2 per cent).

3 Money from the government in a form of tax relief – explained below – at least 0.6 per cent.

From April 2019 the contribution will be 8 per cent of your earnings, that is 4 per cent from you, 3 per cent from your employer and 1 per cent

as tax relief. You may find your employer is more generous and contributes a greater percentage, but they are not legally allowed to be less generous.

You are automatically opted into your work's pension scheme when you join a new company. If you do not want to be part of it, you have to opt out. Avoid doing this, no matter how tempting. Received wisdom is that unless you really cannot afford your life at the moment, perhaps because you are mired in problem debt (remember that loans don't count), you try to stay put. **Opting out of a workplace pension scheme is like turning down a pay rise you are offered for doing no extra work. The money your employer gives you to top up your contribution is 'free', as is the money from the government. It will be so much more expensive to find enough for retirement without this extra cash. Save it or lose it.**

Then there is the fact that it is much easier to save money automatically deducted from your pay packet than it is to resist spending what sits staring at you in your current account.

How pension tax relief works

You do not have to pay tax on any of the money that you put into a pension, up to a point (the point is known as the pension allowance, but I am assuming it is irrelevant for those reading this book, because it is so high: £40,000 a year to a lifetime total of just over £1 million in 2018–2019). This means that if you were to put £100 into a pension it would only actually cost you £80 if you are a basic-rate taxpayer (if you do not understand what kind of taxpayer you are you might want to check out chapter 8 before you read this).

Usually you would pay £20 of that £100 of earnings to the government in income tax. Instead you get the £20 sent back to you and added into a pension pot. You benefit even more if you are a higher-rate taxpayer, where £100 of pension savings would cost you just £60, because usually you pay £40 of that in tax (40 per cent). This tax-relief system is very likely to change, because it is so generous to the richest earners. Sooner or later I think the government will rule that all workers will get the same kind of tax relief. In the meantime if you are a higher earner make the most of the current system.

Final salary vs defined-benefit schemes

You may have heard the term 'gold-plated pensions'. These are for many young people now the stuff of dreams: they are the final-salary or defined-benefit pensions, once called 'the social security miracle of the Western world', that proliferated in the Sixties. You pay into these schemes, but rather than get a pot of money at retirement that you use to draw an income (the size of that income is determined by how big or small your pot is), you get a guaranteed income ever after, calculated as either a proportion of whatever your last salary was at the point at which you retired, or an average of your salary over your career and how long you have been paying in.

These have proved cripplingly expensive for employers as people live longer, so most have shut down or stopped taking new members, particularly in the private sector. Most have been replaced by defined-contribution schemes or 'money-purchase' schemes. These operate as described in the auto-enrolment section and are probably what you have as part of your job package. You pay in a contribution from your salary topped up by your employer and by the government through tax relief. Eventually, when you retire, you will have a pot of savings.

How big the pot is is determined by how much you have put in it over your working life, as well as how much it has grown through investment return.

You can't touch this pot until you are fifty-five. At that age you are free to do a variety of things with it: take out all of it, though this is inadvisable, as it will be taxed heavily; take out a bit of it at a time or take out a quarter of the whole pot, on which you will not pay tax, leaving the rest invested to hopefully grow.

You could take out a lump sum and use the rest to buy an 'annuity', which gives you a 'guaranteed' income every year for the rest of your life. As it is guaranteed the income is often a low one. But you need not worry about these options until you are approaching your fifties, at which point it is a good idea to get financial advice to decide what to do.

Where is my pension pot stashed until retirement?

Part of the problem with engaging with pensions is that it is hard to get a handle on where your money is or what it is doing while you are saving up, because it just comes out of your salary.

Joining the dots helps. Most companies offering defined-contribution pension schemes via auto-enrolment, i.e. the scheme you are most probably in, will choose a pension provider, a massive company often called an insurer, like Scottish Widows or Aviva, to run the pension. That provider will in turn choose fund managers or investment companies (such as Fidelity or Black Rock) who run specific 'funds' into which your pension contribution is invested. These fund managers will pick specific things to split your money between: cash, bonds, and shares of companies you may well have heard of – BT, Shell or Greggs for example.

That means that if you have a pension, and you go into Greggs and eat a sausage roll, or pay BT for a new broadband package, you may actually be supporting a company that you own (though in a very small slice) through your pension. You are invested in the stock market through your workplace pension, even if you do not understand the stock market. How well these companies perform, whether Greggs sells tonnes of sausage rolls, or BT persuades loads of people to sign up to its new BT Sport twenty-four-month exclusive deal, has an impact on how much money is in your pot when you retire. Fund managers try to make as much money as possible for your investment without losing it all, by balancing risks.

There's more information on the world of stocks and shares in chapter 6 to get your head round this.

Why you should move out of the default fund

When you join a workplace pension you will probably be put in a 'default fund', when the provider chooses one fund managed by one company. These type of funds tend, however, to be quite cautious. Greater risk means greater reward when it comes to investment, which means that staying in a default fund, especially when you are in your twenties and thirties, young enough to ride out the ups and downs of the market, is not going to get you as big a pot as a more adventurous fund.

Of the 61 per cent of people who are even aware that they have a workplace pension, 80 per cent stay in the default fund, 95 per cent have never tried to change their fund, 91 per cent do not know where their funds are being invested, and 80 per cent do not know how much money is in their pension pot, according to a report from 2017 called *Damage by Default: the Flaw in Pensions Auto Enrolment*, by behavioural-science consultancy Decision Technology. It says that auto-enrolment has used our tendency towards apathy when it comes to money and saving for the future to discourage people from 'opting out' (by opting them in automatically), but once we are there the same apathy is leaving people losing money by being invested in the wrong funds, £700 a year per employee, by its estimations. All the people I know who are confident about money matters, mostly colleagues at *The Times* such as the investment editor, have switched out of a default pension fund, and even then, the 'experts' were a bit apathetic about it. Everyone finds pensions dry.

Yet most workplaces offer you a large variety of funds to choose from, and working out which looks the most likely to earn you a decent return will make a big difference to how much money you have when you retire, and therefore how much you have to give up now. The same report estimates you could increase your pot by an average of £180,000 by quitting the default fund for something more suited to your circumstances. It concludes: 'employees are blissfully unaware that they could increase their savings with very little effort by simply choosing to move their pension out of the default fund.'

Tom McPhail, head of pensions policy at the investment company Hargreaves Lansdown, and one of the most knowledgeable people on pensions around (he often advises the government on pensions policy), says a default fund is basically the least worst option – better than nothing, but rarely the best.

You may also want to have some power over how your money is being invested for ethical reasons. (Check out the ethical money chapter 12 for more.) Default funds may hold oil companies, for example, and you would rather your own savings did not go towards producing fossil fuels. Most employers will offer an ethical fund which invests your pension in companies that are conscious of social and environmental impact. Speak to your employer about what funds they offer and the process of switching into a different one.

Pensions if you are self-employed

If you are your own boss you cannot take advantage of an employer's contribution, which means saving into a pension is less of a no-brainer. It is still worth trying to set one up yourself, however, to take advantage of the tax breaks and to force yourself into a long-term savings habit. With no employee contributions you are even less likely to be able to afford to retire.

There are three types of pensions you can set up yourself: a personal pension, a stakeholder pension, or a self-invested personal pension (SIPP). The main difference between a personal pension and a stakeholder pension, which can be opened with insurers such as Aviva or Scottish Widows, or investment companies or a high-street bank, is the charges to open one (stakeholder pensions tend to be cheaper, capping how much you pay at 1.5 per cent of the fund's value for the first ten years, 1 per cent after that) and the range of funds on offer – stakeholders can be more restrictive, though you still get a reasonable amount of choice, depending on what company you choose to open a pension with.

A SIPP is more of a DIY pension option. You can invest in almost anything you like – funds, individual shares, commercial property – but that involves more risk and responsibility, and these are better suited to those keen to learn more about investment and put some hours into researching it.

A solid, straightforward option is to take out a personal pension with NEST. This is the National Employment Saving Trust workplace pension scheme created by the government when it launched automatic enrolment. It is used by many companies but is also available to the self-employed. It offers reasonable fees, which work out at about 0.5 per cent for most savers, you can view your account online, stop and start contributions and pay in with your debit card, or via direct debit. There are five funds to choose from, which vary depending on your appetite for risk and any ethical leanings. Another option is the online PensionBee which has annual fees of no more than 0.95 per cent, and you can easily manage it on your phone.

Other people can also contribute to your pension, and you can also set up pensions for children.

If you were in a workplace pension before you went self-employed you may be able to continue to pay into it, even though you will no longer get the employee contribution. This can be a smart option. Many big companies can negotiate lower pension-scheme charges than individuals, so it could work out cheaper than setting up your own new pot.

Should you save in the Lifetime ISA instead?

An alternative to a pension is the Lifetime ISA. This is a savings account to save for a first home and/or retirement, open to anyone under the age of forty. As with other ISAs, you don't pay tax on the returns on your savings. You can put in up to £4,000 a year and will receive a bonus of 25 per cent – that is up to £1,000 – from the government until you are fifty, or until you have used the LISA to buy your first home, whichever is sooner.

You can use the money to buy a home worth a maximum of £450,000, otherwise you cannot take it out before you hit sixty without losing your bonus and some, the equivalent of about 6 per cent of your total pot. This is more flexible than a pension, though, where you cannot take the money out at all before fifty-five. **Savers have the potential to earn a total of £33,000 in bonuses if they pay in the maximum £128,000 from age eighteen until they turn fifty. Accounts can be held in cash, or stocks and shares.**

If you are a higher-rate taxpayer the LISA is not as generous as the tax relief you get on a pension, however.

How much should I save in a pension?

Like working out how much money you should spend on hotels, haircuts, rent (do you want to live in Liverpool or Cornwall, London or Berlin?), deciding how much you need to retire on is totally subjective and based on your own tastes, abilities and circumstances. Some will be happy with a very modest life pottering around garden centres and having cups of tea in the Asda cafe, others will want to spend their twilight years finding themselves in the ashrams of Kerala. To plan how much you should save now for your future, you need to work out roughly what you want (and can afford) that future to look like, and at what age you want it to start. It is a bit tricky to then work out how much to save in today's money, given that your future may be decades away and there is investment return and inflation to consider. Fortunately there are some handy rules of thumb to help.

Obviously rules of thumb are just that, lacking in any nuance and often created by ultra-cautious sorts who work in the financial services industry and live and breathe percentages and insurance, risk and reward. You might have other ways that you expect to fund your retirement – downsizing your home (though this is not risk-free, as house prices can fall as well as rise), an inheritance from parents who you know are not going to need years of residential care. And there's always that mega-hit novel you will write. But for most relying on salary as their only income, they are a useful starting point.

The first is that **you probably want an income in retirement roughly equivalent to half or two-thirds of what you feel comfortable living on at the moment to maintain the same quality of life.** That is because most older people have paid off a mortgage and no longer need to cough up for children or childcare, commuting costs, or colleagues' leaving presents. This is looking a less accurate picture these days, though, with so many young people likely to be still renting into their old age, or paying off mortgages that they could not afford to take out until their forties.

Most people say you want to aim to save for about twenty years of retirement income, which with the current life expectancy of twenty- and thirtysomethings works out as retiring about seventy and dying at ninety. To get to that position you need to save way more than you imagine. Auto-enrolment workplace pensions can lull you into a false sense of security. The contributions stated by law are well below the amount that experts advise you to put away.

Some wealth planners say that you should aim to have at least the equivalent of your annual salary saved for retirement by the time you are thirty, three times that sum by the time you are forty, eight times by the time you are sixty, ten times by retirement, in order to maintain your standard of living. Someone used to all the perks of a £100,000 salary would need to have at least £1 million saved to not feel poorer in retirement.

To have almost £30,000 a year (£20,000 private pension plus £8,500 state pension) to live on in retirement, though this is quite a lot if you no longer have housing costs to worry about, Tom McPhail says a thirty-year-old retiring at sixty-eight would need to save £750 a month to build up a pension pot of £400,000.

Some financial advisers suggest you contribute at least 12.5 per cent to 15 per cent of your salary each month (that includes employer contribution and tax relief), or take the age you start saving for a pension and halve it, and put this percentage of your pre-tax salary aside each year until you retire. You can ask your pension provider for a statement to see how much is already in your pension pot, and an estimate of what that will turn into when you start taking it at retirement.

The best way to work out whether you should save more is to use an online pension calculator – there are many online that operate in the same way. Try the one on the Money Advice Service site. You enter your current age; age when you would like to stop working; salary; how much you are already contributing to a pension, if you are; your target income – i.e. what kind of yearly amount of money you want to live on – and you can see on a sliding scale how much you need to be saving to meet it based on certain assumptions, like the rate of inflation and investment returns. Read it and weep.

Where are my old pensions?

The average person has worked for 5.8 employers by the time they are fifty-five, but this is going to rise significantly over the next decades. According to the investment and financial planning firm Tilney Group, eighteen- to 34-year-olds have already had on average over four jobs, The Department of Work & Pensions estimates the average person will have eleven employers over their working lives. That is a lot of little pension pots scattered across the UK. How can you keep track of them and what should you do with them all?

Research by Tilney Group also estimates that 7 million people have lost at least one of their pension pots. Among the reasons cited: 'never kept an interest', 'lost paperwork', 'forgotten to notify providers of address changes'.

You can find old pensions you have lost track of using the government's pension-tracing service (gov.uk/find-pension-contact-details), a database of contact details for past and present pension schemes.

If you have lots of little pots it might make sense to consolidate them all into one new plan, maybe with your existing employer, maybe in a separate private pension you set up yourself. This also makes it easier to keep control of how and where your money is invested, what fees you are paying and how much more you need to save. You need to check before you do, though, that you will not be charged big exit penalties: if you are only transferring very small sums it might not be worth it.

PensionBee is an online service that will find your old pensions and consolidate them into one of a choice of its investment plans, 'tracker', 'tailored' or 'future world plan', run by wealth managers BlackRock, State Street or Legal & General. All come with low fees and are super-easy to view and keep track of online or on your phone. You will also be warned if moving your old pension could result in large penalties or loss of any benefits.

8

Everything you need to know about tax

You know you have to pay tax, but how much do you really *know* about paying tax? If you are anything like me, I would hazard probably not much – it just comes off your salary. It was not until I went self-employed and had to figure out the dreaded tax return (which is actually, if you have straightforward finances, not as arduous as people led me to believe, but more on that later), that I really understood the fundamentals. This is even though I had, by that point, watched half a dozen Budgets.

The Budget, for the uninitiated, is where the chancellor of the exchequer lays out how he (there has thus far never been a she) is going to tax us all and where that tax is going to be spent. The tax system is inarguably a bitch to understand, and chancellors love to make it so in order to hide how much we are actually paying. Ask any money or business journalist about the manic few hours immediately after the chancellor sits down from making his speech. This is when the multi-page document gets uploaded onto the gov.uk website and you have to pore through it to find the small print, where the government has hidden the ways in which it is actually collecting your cash.

Trying to get your head around the main taxes we pay, and whether they are always due, can save you a lot of money, however. Even if you are not Gary Barlow, there are lots of legitimate ways to avoid tax that are actually promoted by the government. Tax evasion is the illegal one (for example, not declaring your full earnings on a tax return), tax avoidance the non-illegal but sometimes morally dubious one (e.g. accounts that involve the Cayman Islands and 'vehicles' that do not have wheels). For us normals, tax 'reliefs' and allowances are in place to incentivize you to do certain things that society values: save for a pension, start your own business, get married, rear a child, cycle to work, drive a low-emissions car, donate to charity, rent out your spare room, or care for an elderly relative.

Some reliefs and allowances are automatic, but if you do not know about the others then you will not get them, so every year millions of people miss out on valuable benefits. Her Majesty's Revenue & Customs (HMRC) is not going to check that you are claiming all the benefits you are entitled to, or paying the right amount of tax. Correction: Her Majesty's Revenue & Customs is not going to check that you are paying too much tax. You will be chased if you are not paying enough. It is all, as Mr Barlow – or at least Mr Barlow's accountant – knows, about being proactive.

Here are the taxes you are most likely paying, and reliefs you are most likely going to want to make the most of. Important to understand before we start is that many taxes and reliefs apply to a specific year known as the tax year. This is not the same as a calendar year but runs from 6 April until the following 5 April.

Income tax and the personal allowance

Most people pay income tax on any money they earn. The majority of working-age people earn money primarily through their salary, but some also receive income from renting out a property, returns on their savings and investments, or profits from a business that they run. The tax is known as a 'progressive' one, in so far as the more income you earn, the more tax you have to pay. Certain taxes, such as VAT – see below – are not progressive because everyone pays them at the same rate no matter how much money they earn, which means that low earners pay out a larger fraction of their income on such taxes: £10 or 10 per cent of £100, to a minimum-wage cleaner means a lot more than £10 or 10 per cent of £100 does to Richard Branson.

Income tax is paid based on three thresholds, or as they are known 'marginal rates': basic-rate taxpayers owe 20 per cent tax, higher-rate taxpayers 40 per cent, and additional-rate taxpayers 45 per cent. These percentages, plus what income 'bracket' they apply to (the point at which they start getting charged), are set by the government and can be changed on a political whim, though they rarely are, for fear that the electorate will go bananas about paying more income tax (or rich people getting away with paying less).

Everyone has a personal allowance. This is an amount of money you can earn before you pay tax. It too is set by the government. When George Osborne became chancellor in 2010 the personal allowance was £6,475. He pledged to raise it every year; ideologically, Conservatives tend to favour people paying less tax. In the tax year April 2018 to April 2019 the allowance is £11,850, and it is expected to rise to £12,500 by 2020. That means that you owe no income tax at all until you earn £11,850, so that some very low-paid or part-time workers do not have to pay income tax.

Lots of people make the mistake of thinking that basic-rate taxpayers pay 20 per cent on all of their earnings, higher-rate taxpayers pay 40 per cent on all of their earnings. Not so. Those who earn above £11,850 but less than £46,351 pay 20 per cent tax on the difference. Higher-rate taxpayers who earn more than £46,350 will also pay 20 per cent on the sum between the personal allowance (£11,850) and the higher-rate threshold (£46,351), but then 40 per cent on anything above that up to a maximum of £150,000.

Those that earn above £100,000 do, however, lose the personal allowance incrementally: it is reduced by £1 for every £2 you earn over £100,000. Additional-rate taxpayers pay 20 per cent on earnings to £46,351, 40 per cent on earnings to £150,000, and 45 per cent on anything they earn above £150,000.

Some interesting stats for you. **The vast majority of people in the UK pay tax at the basic rate, 81.8 per cent (or 25.1 million people) in 2017; only 13.7 per cent of earners paid higher-rate tax (4.2 million people); and just 1.2 per cent paid additional rate (364,000 people). The top 1 per cent of taxpayers had a 12 per cent share of total income, and were liable for 27.7 per cent of all income tax.**

• •

National Insurance

National Insurance is not technically a tax, though it might as well be, because you have no choice but to pay it if you are working. People therefore often refer to it as a 'stealth tax'. It is instead a social insurance scheme in which while you have a job you pay into a government fund that goes to compensate you if and when you do not. A slice of National Insurance contributions (NICs) pays for the NHS, and the rest is in the National Insurance Fund which is used for mostly state pensions (see more on this in the pensions chapter), unemployment benefits, statutory sick pay, maternity allowance, and so on. **National Insurance is however 'pay as you go'. The contributions you pay are used to fund people needing state benefits immediately, so your NICs are funding your parents' and grandparents' pensions, not yours.**

There are different 'classes' of National Insurance depending on your employment status. You pay varying percentages according to how much you earn. The percentages are calculated on your 'gross' pay, which is the money you receive before income tax is deducted. If you have an employer or are self-employed but have a boss, you pay Class 1 National Insurance. Bosses have to pay employer National Insurance contributions for their workers, too. As with income tax, there is a threshold under which you do not have to pay National Insurance: £8,424 a year for the year 2018–2019. You pay 12 per cent of your earnings on anything above that threshold up to £46,350. On any earnings above £46,350 a year you pay 2 per cent.

If you are self-employed there are two types of National Insurance – class 2 and class 4. You pay class 2 as a flat rate of £2.95 a week (true of 2018–2019). You can choose not to pay this if your profits are below a threshold of £6,205 (true of 2018–2019). If your profits are above £8,424 (true of 2018–2019) you have to pay class 4 contributions, which amount to 9 per cent of profits between £8,424 and £46,350. You pay 2 per cent of anything over that.

You may want to pay voluntary National Insurance contributions, which are known as class 3, if you are unable to work for a period of time through sickness or childcare, or because you are working overseas for a foreign employer, for example (see pensions chapter for more on this). You need a certain amount of NICs to be eligible for some benefits, such as the state pension. These cost £14.65 a week.

Understand your payslip and tax code

There are a lot of random letters relating to tax, just to add to the general nightmarishness of it. Here are the ones that you need to know:

PAYE stands for pay as you earn, and is the way you will pay tax if you are employed (for those that are self-employed skip on). Your employer will pay income tax and National Insurance to HMRC on your behalf before you receive your salary. How much that is is set out in your payslip, which is essentially a receipt for your earnings, income tax and National Insurance.

Most people get a payslip monthly but it depends how frequently you get paid. Your payslip states your gross pay and net pay. I always forget the difference and remind myself that gross can mean big, so the bigger amount. Your gross pay is how much you receive before tax. This is generally what you would consider to be your salary, i.e. if you are on £30,000 that is £30,000 gross. Net pay is what goes into your bank account once income tax and National Insurance have been deducted.

Your **P60** is the form you receive at the end of each tax year with a summary of your total pay and total tax and National Insurance deducted. Keep hold of this in case any questions about your tax crop up in future years.

A **P45** is a form that is issued if you leave your job and shows how much tax you have paid in the year to that point. You keep part of it and give part of it to your employer in any new job you take on.

You are assigned a tax code by HMRC which will also appear on your payslip. This is the code that

indicates to employers how much tax to deduct via PAYE. You should check this especially when you start a new job, because the onus is on you to ensure that your tax code is correct – no one else is going to tell you. If it is wrong you could be paying too much, or too little.

You may be on an emergency tax code. This often happens if your new employer does not have your P45. Most emergency tax codes end with **M1** or **W1**, which indicates that you are being taxed monthly or weekly rather than annually, or maybe **0T**, which indicates that you do not get the personal allowance because HMRC does not have enough information about your income.

You are most likely to be on a tax code that ends in an **L**, which applies to those who have one job and claim no taxable benefits. Generally the rule is that you multiply the number in your tax code by ten to get the amount of money you can earn each year before being taxed, so at the moment, while the personal allowance is £11,850, your tax code will read 1185L. You can check if yours is correct on HMRC's online income-tax checker (gov.uk/check-income-tax-current-year).

Your payslip will also detail any pension contributions and deductions made from your gross pay, and any student loan. Your student loan comes out of your gross pay automatically, so you do not need to do anything about it unless you are self-employed, explained below.

● ●

Tax reliefs and allowances

Tax reliefs are amounts of money for certain things the government likes that you can deduct from your gross pay, so you do not have to pay tax on them. Think of them as like a boost to your personal allowance. Here are some of the reliefs you are most likely to need to know about.

Pensions

Any money you pay into a pension product, whether that is through your workplace pension scheme or in a private pension you set up yourself, is tax-free (up to a very generous point that you do not really need to know about unless you are extremely wealthy or close to retirement). That means that for every £1 you save into a pension it actually only costs you 80p, if you are a basic-rate taxpayer, 60p if you are a higher-rate taxpayer, and 55p if you are an additional-rate taxpayer. More on this in the pension chapter.

Charity giving

Some companies offer payroll charity-giving schemes or 'give as you earn', where your contribution to charity is taken off your gross pay so that you do not pay tax on it. When you sponsor someone's 10km or sign up for a monthly charity direct debit, the charity will apply to HMRC to get back the tax you've already paid on. So that's why your donation will actually be more generous than the sum you give, i.e. if you donated £10 the charity actually gets £12 if you are a basic-rate taxpayer. This is how gift aid works. If you are a higher-rate taxpayer you need to claim back the additional 20 per cent, either by filling out a self-assessment tax return or calling HMRC.

Rent-a-room scheme and Airbnb

If you are fortunate enough to own your own home with a spare room and you want to rent it out or put it on Airbnb, you can earn up to £7,500 (in 2018–2019) in rental income before you have to pay any income tax on it. However, from April 2019 this is only the case if you are around for at least some of your Airbnb guest's stay. You will have to pay income tax if you earn money from Airbnb while you are on holiday yourself for example.

You can also earn up to £1,000 tax-free from your property, for example by renting out your driveway or parking space.

Cycle-to-work scheme

You can save as much as 42 per cent, for higher-rate taxpayers, and 32 per cent as a basic-rate taxpayer, on a bike to use for commuting to work via the cycle-to-work scheme. Your employer pays the cost of the bike and you pay your company back in instalments as a 'salary sacrifice', i.e. money that comes out of your gross pay automatically. That means you are not paying tax on it, unlike if you were to buy a bike out of your net pay. You can spend up to £1,000 on a bike and equipment. Check out bike2workscheme.co.uk for more.

ISAs and the personal savings allowance

You pay income tax on income that you earn from your savings, for example through interest paid on a cash account, or from dividends paid on investments. ISAs are savings accounts into which you can save a specific amount per year (£20,000 in the tax year 2018–2019). Any interest earned on cash ISAs, or any investment return earned from stocks and shares ISAs, is tax-free.

Now, however, there is also a personal savings allowance. This is a sum of money you can earn in interest on any kind of savings account before you have to pay tax. Unless you have loads of savings, it is more than sufficient: £1,000 if you are a basic-rate taxpayer, and £500 if you are a higher-rate taxpayer. Additional-rate taxpayers do not get a personal savings allowance.

Investment returns

If you invest outside of an ISA you are liable to pay tax on profits you make, income tax on dividends, and capital-gains tax (see more below) on any rise in value of shares you sell. You are unlikely to have to do so though, because you get a generous yearly capital-gains tax allowance, currently £11,700 (in 2018–2019) each year. You can earn £2,000 from dividends (for 2018–2019) without paying tax.

Marriage allowance

The existing government rewards couples for being married with various tax breaks. The marriage allowance can save you £238 a year, but few people actually claim it – 2.2 million couples of the 4.4 million couples eligible have failed to ask for the money since it was introduced in 2015. To qualify, one of you in a married couple must be earning less than the personal allowance in a particular tax year – that is not paying any tax at all. The other partner must be a basic-rate taxpayer. The earning partner can transfer £1,190 of their personal allowance to their spouse, which reduces the earning partner's tax bill. This is a good perk even if you are only temporarily earning under the personal allowance; maybe you are on shared parental leave, for example.

The marriage allowance came in in April 2015. If you were eligible back then but did not realize you can claim backdated payments.

When you are married you can share assets, so if you have lots of savings, or may earn income on a property, for example, and one of a couple earns less than the other – say one is a basic-rate taxpayer and the other a higher-rate taxpayer – you can juggle your assets so that they are in the name of the basic-rate taxpayer and therefore take advantage of a higher personal-savings allowance.

Childcare

Parents can claim up to £2,000 a year tax-free per child (or £4,000 for disabled children) aged under eleven (or under seventeen for disabled children), to pay for childcare. To qualify both parents must be working and earning at least £125.28 a week, and no one partner can earn more than £100,000 a year. Self-employed people can also take advantage of this. There is no earnings limit for freelancers. You have to register and open an online account with the government to get the allowance. The government tops up every £8 you pay in with £2, up to a maximum of £2,000 per child per year.

Self-employment and tax

If you are self-employed you are entitled to all of the above tax reliefs and some but you will have to detail them on a self-assessment tax return.

You have to tell HMRC as soon as you become self-employed and fill out your own tax return via self-assessment in order to calculate how much income tax and National Insurance you will have to pay. It is easiest to file your return online detailing your income for the tax year that ended on the previous April. The deadline for online returns is 31 January each year, so for example you would fill out a tax return for the year 5 April 2017 to 6 April 2018 by 31 January 2019. If you have a turnover of more than £85,000 you also have to register for VAT.

The difficulty with doing tax yourself is that you have to make sure you save enough to cover it, otherwise you are in trouble, and, as sometimes happens to celebs, if you do not you might end up going bankrupt. To work out how much you are likely to owe, based on how much you are likely to earn in the next year, you can use the self-assessment ready reckoner online at gov.uk/self-assessment-ready-reckoner.

Not only do you have to pay any tax due for the previous tax year, but you also have to pay advance payments towards next year's tax bill, of roughly half of what it is expected to be – this is due at the end of July.

For most self-employed freelancers you will use 'cash basis' accounting. This is where you declare money you received, or spent on expenses, pensions and so on, in that particular tax year. As a freelance journalist, for example, I do not have to declare any money pending on articles I have written but have not yet been paid for. You need to tot up what you have earned, as well as any business expenses which are tax-deductible, mentioning any other ways you have used your money that year – saving for a pension, giving to charity – that may enable you to save more tax. This will be taken off your income total and the remainder is what is taxed. I find it easiest to do this by printing out all my bank statements and getting happy with different-coloured highlighter pens.

If you have a student loan you need to also say so on your self-assessment form, and HMRC will calculate how much you have to repay based on your earnings that year.

I'm self-employed, what business expenses can I claim?

You can offset quite a bit against tax and save a significant sum every year as a result, ranging from the calls you make for work to a proportion of your heating if you work from home.

If there are things you use for both your job and personal life, however, you need to work out what percentage of time and money is spent using it for work. HMRC points out that if you have the same mobile phone for business and pleasure, you need to divide up your bill. It uses the example of a £200 a year mobile bill, of which £130 is spent on personal calls and £70 on business: you can claim only £70 on business as allowable expenses. It might be more straightforward to get a work mobile, and then you can expense the whole monthly contract fee or pay-as-you-go bills, as well as the cost of the handset. If you were to buy a new iPhone for £1,000 you could add £1,000 to the expenses total on your self-assessment form, and if you are a basic-rate taxpayer it would actually cost you only £800. Similarly you can claim for any other office equipment, such as a new laptop, any stationery, postage, printing and computer software.

You can also claim for the cost of the office. If you work in a co-working space you would enter the amount you pay for renting a desk, for example. If you work from home you can claim part of your heating and electricity bill, your council tax, mortgage interest or rent, or broadband and phone bill. It is not the easiest thing to work out exactly what proportion of all of that is used while you are working. You could potentially figure out how many rooms you use for business, or the amount of time you spend working from home.

HMRC's example is if you have four rooms in your home, one is an office, and your electricity bill is £400 a year, you could argue that each room uses equal amounts of electricity, so you could claim £100 a year for expenses. If you work at home one day a week in that office you would divide that £100 by seven, and claim £14.29.

HMRC offers a 'flat-rate' option, known as simplified expenses, to make things a bit more straightforward. This is £10 a month if you work at home between twenty-five and fifty hours a week, up to £26 a month if you work 101 hours or more. These do not include broadband and phone costs though, which you have to work out separately. You can also use flat rates to work out car mileage for work travel of 45p per mile for any cars you drive for the first 10,000 miles, 25p thereafter. Use the gov.uk simplified expenses online calculator to figure out whether you are better off with flat rates or doing the maths yourself.

You can claim for any travel you do for work – flights or train tickets and parking costs – but you cannot claim for travelling to and from your office, so bus fares to your co-working space are out. You can claim for any uniform you have to wear, but sadly not for a new capsule work wardrobe so that you look great in meetings. You cannot claim for taking clients out for coffee in the name of schmoozing, but website costs, magazine or newspaper subscriptions that you need for work, or the cost of hiring a lawyer or accountant, are all fine.

For a more comprehensive insight see the gov.uk site self-employed expenses section.

You need to keep a record of all of your expenses for at least five years. You do not have to show your records when you fill out your self-assessment form; all that is required is one figure

total for how much your expenses amount to in that tax year, but you may be called up by HMRC to show that your expenses are correct. Records include receipts and bank statements.

There are some handy apps and bank accounts to help you file as you go, such as Expensify and Coconut, which recognizes your expenses and automatically files receipts. Starling, Revolut and Monzo all let you tag expenses and keep receipts.

I'm self-employed, do I need an accountant?

If you are worried about what expenses you can or cannot claim, or making any mistake on your self-assessment form, you might want to hire an accountant. You also have a bit more protection if HMRC was to investigate your tax affairs, though ultimately the burden of responsibility for your tax affairs being correct and proper lies with you the individual – you cannot palm it off on someone else.

Is it worth the money? Karen Barrett, founder of the website Unbiased, which is a good place to look for a trustworthy local accountant, says you should hire one when it becomes less costly than handling your accounts yourself. To work this out, **estimate how much an hour of your time is worth, by dividing your monthly income by the number of hours you work each month. Then estimate how much of your time is spent on managing your accounts. If the result is more than £60 per month, a lowish fee for small businesses, then get a professional to do it.**

Other taxes worth knowing about

VAT

You pay Value Added Tax (VAT) on goods and services you buy that are considered 'luxuries' rather than necessities, though this definition is very dubious – biscuits coated in caramel or icing are VAT-free, biscuits coated in chocolate are not.

VAT is generally hidden in prices in shops, or restaurants and hotels (unlike in the US, where tax sneaks up on you). VAT is currently 20 per cent for everyone, which is why, as previously mentioned, it is not considered progressive, because those who have less money end up contributing a higher proportion of their income in VAT. Watch out for when you are buying something from a small business, however; they may add VAT on afterwards. This caught me out a lot last year when I got married and realized all the reasonable enough quotations for anything wedding-related, such as the catering, were way lower than I would eventually pay once 20 per cent was added on.

There are some funny VAT anomalies. For example, you do not pay VAT on cold takeaway food, such as sandwiches, but you do pay VAT on cold food like sandwiches that are eaten in, which is why you have to pay more to eat in in Pret.

Stamp duty

If you are buying a home you have to pay stamp-duty tax on the new property unless you are a first-time buyer buying a property under £300,000. There's more on this in chapter 2.

Inheritance tax

You are taxed on the transfer of everything you own to someone else when you die. Of course you are no longer around to pay the tax, so the tax comes out of what you have left behind: your estate. There is an inheritance-tax threshold below which no tax is owed, currently £325,000. This is called the nil-rate band.

If your home or assets are worth more than this nil-rate band, tax is charged on anything above it at 40 per cent. Married couples have a combined £650,000 nil-rate band, as long as the first in the couple to die leaves their whole estate to their spouse.

There is a new additional allowance for 'residences', i.e. houses, up to £125,000 each (a further £250,000 as a married couple) if you are passing your home on to direct descendants – that is either your children or grandchildren. This means that if your married parents die you will have to pay inheritance tax on any house you inherit only if it is worth more than £900,000.

Married couples do not have to pay inheritance tax on estates they inherit from each other, but cohabiting couples might (read chapter 10 for more).

You can give people gifts of money, but they will be liable for inheritance tax if you die within seven years. You do get a £3,000-a-year gift allowance, however. On top of this you can give money gifts for a wedding or civil partnership of up to £5,000 to each of your children and their intended partner, up to £2,500 for each grandchild, or £1,000 to anyone else, for example a nephew or niece or close friend, without them attracting inheritance tax.

Capital gains tax

You pay capital gains tax (CGT) when you sell an asset that has increased in value. The 'gain' in value is taxed at 28 per cent on your gains from residential property and 20 per cent on other assets, such as shares, if you are a higher-rate taxpayer. Everyone gets a tax-free allowance of up to £11,700 for CGT, so you only pay it on any gains above that. The most likely reason you will pay CGT at a young age is if, remarkably, you own more than one property. You do not pay CGT on your main home, but it is owed if you sell a second holiday home, or a buy-to-let.

I have written this book for people on average or above-average salaries in particular, so I will not go into all the benefits available to those on low incomes. There are many, and they are notoriously complicated, and whether or not you get them depends on lots of factors. If you are a very low earner, or if you are unwell or disabled, you should investigate whether you are eligible. Try the website for the charity Turn2Us which has a useful benefits calculator.

You do however get some benefits if you earn above-average salaries.

● ●

Benefits you should claim if you are a parent, or about to be one

Child benefit

Most people can claim child benefit for any child that is either theirs, or that they look after, if the child is under sixteen, or if they are under twenty but in full-time education or training. **You get £20.70 a week for your first child and £13.70 a week for any subsequent children, which amounts to more than £1,000 a year for one child, and an extra £700 per next child. You need to actively claim it, and you should claim it as soon as your child is born, because payments can**

only be backdated three months from the date your application is received. Download a form from gov.uk to do so.

If you or your partner earn over £60,000 you do not get child benefit, but you can claim it and then pay it back in extra income tax. Your circumstances might make this worth doing, and an accountant can help you decide. If either of you earn between £50,000 and £60,000 you need to pay back 1 per cent of the child benefit for every £100 income you earn over £50,000 via a self-assessment tax return.

Claiming child benefit automatically entitles you to National Insurance credits towards your state pension (see chapter 7 for why this is important). Be alert, therefore, to the fact that if you are not claiming child benefit because you or your partner is a high earner you are not getting these credits, and may not receive the full state pension unless you fill the gaps.

Shared parental leave, maternity and paternity pay

If you or your partner are having a baby or adopting, you are legally entitled to time off work and some pay for up to a year afterwards. You also have the legal right to paid time off work to go to any antenatal appointments, in addition to your annual leave. A pregnant woman's partner is entitled to take unpaid leave to go to two antenatal appointments with her.

Statutory maternity pay is offered to any pregnant woman who is employed and earns at least £116 a week, and has been working for her employer for at least twenty-six weeks. If the above does not apply, or you are self-employed, you get maternity allowance.

You are legally entitled to take up to fifty-two weeks' maternity leave, during which you get thirty-nine weeks of statutory maternity pay. It breaks down as 90 per cent of your average weekly earnings before tax for the first six weeks, followed by the lower of either £145.18, or 90 per cent of your average weekly earnings for the next thirty-three weeks. The remaining thirteen weeks if taken would be unpaid. Your employer may offer you a more generous package, but this is the minimum you must get. To claim it you need to tell your boss when you want to stop working by the fifteenth week before the baby is due.

Maternity allowance is £145.18 a week, or 90 per cent of your average weekly earnings (whichever is less) for thirty-nine weeks, then £27 a week for fourteen weeks.

The partner of the mother is entitled to two weeks' paid time off work as long as you have worked for your employer for twenty-six weeks by the fifteenth week before the baby is due, and earn at least £116 a week. This amounts to the same as statutory maternity pay, £145.18 a week or 90 per cent of your average weekly earnings, whichever is lower. The thirty-nine weeks of maternity pay or maternity allowance, and the fifty-two weeks of maternity leave, are now transferrable as shared parental pay and leave. So each parent could take half each, or if, for example, the pregnant mum is self-employed, the full-time employee partner could claim the full allowance and take the full fifty-two weeks' leave.

Unfortunately, take-up of this has been unbelievably low – just 2 per cent of couples in the three years since it has been launched. Part of the issue is that many employers pay pregnant mums better than statutory maternity pay, but will not pay fathers, or partners of new mothers,

as much, so it makes more financial sense for the partner to go back to work.

Note that if you are pregnant you also get free NHS dental care and free prescriptions, lasting until a year after the baby is born.

9
Understand your bills and insurance

There is such a thing as too much choice. Last time I checked (and the number has probably already crept up), there were 4,987 different insurance policies available for you to pick from. That is over 1,200 more than there were in 2015, and almost 4,000 more than in 2003, according to money analyst Defaqto.

This number includes 976 separate annual travel-insurance policies and 952 single-trip travel-insurance policies; 159 to cover mobile phone and gadgets and 721 car-breakdown policies all offered by 1,579 different insurance 'providers'. There were just 560 such providers in 2003.

That is just the exciting world of insurance. While there was once a rule that limited energy companies (of which there are now more than sixty, and counting) to offering just four different tariffs each, now there is no end to what they can try and sell you in the name of 'tailoring' to your specific energy needs.

Want a new mobile phone and broadband? Which of the HALF A MILLION – no joke – exclusive deals do you fancy? Don't get me started on how many comparison sites there are, which one is any good. Hang on, who is comparing the comparison sites? Some comparison sites work on the completely-useless-to-customers basis that the company that pays the highest commission gets bumped the highest up the 'best buy' tables, while other genuinely best buys do not even make an appearance.

Like a particularly taxing game of splat the rat, financial services companies are forever popping up and disappearing only to then rebrand, offering hundreds of different subtle tweaks on some fundamental household utility or service that we all need but find extremely tedious and confusing to buy. Many companies offer a 'white label' product, where a small new company, such as thebestvalueinsurancehonestly.com buys the services of a big well-known brand, and repackages them as something 'new', when really you are buying exactly what you would buy if you bought directly through the familiar brand; just scroll to the ultra-small greyed-out wording at the bottom of its website and you can usually see what big company is behind it.

The market for financial products is, as a result, arse-achingly complex, and a huge effort to navigate.

This means you are almost certainly spending more money than you need to be, because who is going to sit down and work out the pros and cons of 1,928 different travel-insurance policies to find the absolute cheapest for you? I know this is the worst, most expensive, idea ever, and yet I have bought travel insurance from some screen in Gatwick airport just before I boarded a plane because I forgot my last policy had run out.

Unfortunately, many insurers, mobile networks, energy companies – on it goes – punish customer inertia, which means that 'shopping around', loathsome phrase as it is, will almost certainly result in you saving several hundred pounds, possibly pushing £1,000 each year.

There is a more than £370 annual difference between the most expensive and the cheapest energy tariff on the market according to energyhelpline.com, from companies offering you essentially the same thing, the ability to heat and light your home. Recent research found that a 'loyal' insurance customer, i.e. one that sticks with the same company and lets their insurance policy roll on year after year, will, after five years, find themselves paying 75 per cent more

than a new customer would for exactly the same insurance cover.

I have seen dozens of readers lose out by thousands of pounds over years for making the mistake of believing that because they are 'loyal' to a brand they will be paying what the market says it is worth to insure their home or car. The companies invariably argue that, well, they could have gone elsewhere. But what do you actually need? And what tricks to avoid getting ripped off? This chapter is about how to read your household bills and insurance, understand what you are paying for, and whether or not you really need it, so you can pick the best-value deal as quickly as possible and get on with your life.

● ●

Energy

What's on my bill?

The most lucrative way to reduce your energy consumption, and therefore your bills, is to turn down the thermostat. Dropping it by just 1°C can cut heating bills by up to £75 a year, according to the Energy Saving Trust. But you will save much more by picking a cheaper tariff than the one you are on at the moment if you signed up to your existing tariff more than a couple of years ago, or without giving it much thought. Your tariff is how much you have to pay for a unit of energy, measured as a kilowatt per hour of gas or electricity, plus an additional standing charge which is essentially the admin fee you pay to your energy company to have your energy supplied.

At the moment energy companies can price their tariffs as they like. The idea is that competition in the marketplace between them all keeps prices affordable, because people will just vote with their feet if they are paying too much, right? But from the end of 2018 the government is going to cap how much they can push up their 'standard variable rate' products, after the appalling scandal of fuel poverty, where elderly people are literally dying of the cold because they cannot afford to heat their homes. **The standard variable rate (SVR) is the price of a 'default' tariff, which, as the name suggests, varies and is usually the most expensive deal. A remarkable number of people sit on these, 57 per cent of energy customers, according to**

uswitch, paying way more than they need to as the cost of energy creeps up.

Price rises are often justified by the rising cost of 'wholesale energy': energy companies have to bulk-buy natural gas or electricity before they offer it on to customers.

So first things first, you are generally best not being on a company's standard variable rate. If you are, move off it pronto. Look for a fixed-rate tariff where you pay a fixed price per unit of energy. These tend to be cheapest and protect you from sudden price rises. When picking one check for exit fees, though. Some fixed-rate deals do not have exit fees, which means you can change deals whenever you like without paying a penalty if more affordable ones appear.

Always opt for an online tariff, agreeing to accept paperless billing and input meter readings online, which are generally cheaper, and less hassle, anyway.

If you do not mind running your washing machine in the middle of the night, you could go for the time-of-use tariff offered by some energy companies, where you get a cheaper price for electricity you use when there is lower demand on the National Grid. British Gas's HomeEnergy gives customers free electricity on a Saturday. If you use both electricity and gas from the same supplier, get yourself on a 'dual fuel' tariff where you get both on the same deal. Again, this is significantly cheaper than buying both separately, though possibly more expensive than getting gas from one supplier and electricity from another.

Make sure you pay by direct debit; you get a discount for doing so.

Check you are not paying energy based on estimated meter readings – your bill will show an E next to your consumption figures if you are. Take meter readings and send them to your supplier, otherwise you could end up paying too much for a long time or, possibly worse, way too little only to be hit with an unexpectedly massive bill further down the line when the figures are corrected.

Smart meters automatically monitor your energy use and send it to your supplier. They also have a screen that shows you exactly how many pennies you are spending every time you have a shower or boil the kettle – quite unsettling, ripe to trigger snippy comments from your other half who does not see why you can't just put another jumper on, but a useful way to count them if you are on a tight budget.

Smart meters are being rolled out by all suppliers free, though the cost will be swallowed by raising all customers' energy bills. They have been criticised, however, because the first roll-out of them is non-transferable. That means if you have one installed while you are with British Gas it becomes redundant if you then switch to E.ON. Check before having one installed.

Smart tariffs, for those that have a smart meter, may, like time-of-use tariffs, offer you a discount for energy you use at unusual times. Some energy suppliers keen to encourage people to sign up for smart meters are offering cheaper tariffs to smart meter users. Better could be a smart thermostat like Nest which learns your routine and turns heating on and off when you are not using it, works with smart switches to warn you that you left all the lights on, and sends you a report analysing usage.

Water

Unlike energy, you cannot switch water suppliers, you are stuck with whoever operates in your area. You can still shave some money off your bills, though.

You pay for water in one of two ways in England and Wales. Your bill is either based on the 'rateable value' of your home, which is loosely related to its size and value (but this hasn't been updated for decades), which is a fixed cost of water multiplied by your home's rateable value, plus a standing charge, which is basically an admin charge for processing and issuing bills, answering customer-service calls etc. Or your home is metered and you pay depending on how much water you use, as well as the standing charge.

In this case you are charged for water in 'cubic metres', that is 1,000 litres of water, the equivalent, according to United Utilities the water company, of 13 baths, 14 washing machine loads, 28 showers, 111 loo flushes or 3,300 cups of tea. Each cubic metre costs about £3. You then pay for wastewater or sewage to be taken away from your home (when it drains or flushes), in a sewage charge per cubic metre, plus a surface-water charge, which is a fixed amount for dealing with the water that drains off your home into public sewers. If you live in a very rural home you might have a 'soakaway', or your surface water may run into a stream, in which case you should not be paying surface-water charge and you should ask to have this taken off your bill.

If you live in Scotland your water bill is based on your council-tax band, and it costs money to have a meter installed, so you are better off not doing so. In England and Wales, however, you could potentially cut your bills dramatically by installing a meter, free, if you do not have one already.

Usually, if you have more or the same number of bedrooms than the number of people using them – say you live alone, or are a couple with a one- or two-bedroom house – it is cheaper to get a meter. You can use an online calculator such as the one offered by the Consumer Council for Water, or your water company, to check whether it is going to save you.

Sometimes a property is not suitable for a meter; often this happens in blocks of flats. If this is the case ask your water company for an 'assessed tariff', which is an assessment of how much water you are likely to use if you were on a meter. If you live alone and cannot fit a meter you may be able to apply for a single-occupancy tariff, which will lower your bills. Some water companies offer special tariffs for low users which have no standing charge, but a higher charge per cubic metre of water used.

You can get free water-saving gadgets from your water company. This includes water-regulating shower heads, tap inserts, and bags you put in your loo cistern to reduce the amount you use every time you flush, which could chip an extra chunk off your annual bill.

Broadband

Always try to move broadband supplier, or negotiate price, at the end of your contract period – usually after eighteen months. The comparison site uswitch reports that you may be charged as much as double if you do not bother. One of my colleagues told me she had just noticed her Virgin Media package had gone up from £23 to £35 a month after her initial contract came to an end. She was paying £12 a month more for exactly the same thing, just because she was no longer a new customer and the enticing discount added to her first year's package had fallen away. She was not alerted when her contract came to an end, of course. There may soon be rules that broadband companies have to notify customers but until then you need to put a notification in your calendar to remind you to switch, otherwise you'll keep rolling on, paying more and more.

Many do not move because the thought of being without internet is too stressful, but you should not be without internet for more than an hour or two. Generally the switching process is smooth and worth giving a go. Read on for how, though first a bit of background on the types of broadband available.

Most broadband in the UK uses ADSL (Asymmetric Digital Subscriber Line), which is the connection provided through copper telephone lines from a telephone exchange. The UK's phone-line infrastructure is owned by BT Openreach, so you need to rent a line from BT to access it. A few years ago broadband companies would advertise their nice affordable monthly prices neglecting to add on the monthly cost you are obliged to pay BT for a landline (about £20 a month). Now they have to advertise total costs including this landline rental.

Broadband speed is measured in bits, kilobits (Kbps or Kb), megabits (Mbps or Mb) or gigabits per second (Gbps or Gb). With ADSL, download speeds are limited to 17 Mbps, but could be much less if you live far away from the nearest telephone exchange: longer wire means slower speeds. You can check online to see how far away your nearest telephone exchange is from your postcode. Try the site thinkbroadband.com.

So-called 'superfast' broadband uses fibre-optic cables. Most use a fibre connection to connect the telephone exchange to the cabinet in your street and then use a phone line for the rest of the journey to your home. This is called 'fibre to the cabinet', or 'FTTC', and offers speeds of up to 76 Mbps, but is not available all over the country. A very small proportion of homes can get the mega-FTTH, fibre to the home, or FTTP, fibre to the premises, which gives you fibre cables directly from the exchange into your home, so you can get speeds of up to 1 Gbps and spend the rest of your days playing ultra-high-definition VR online games.

Virgin Media does not use BT Openreach but has its own fibre-optic cables that connect from the phone exchange to its own street cabinets, and then its own coaxial cables into your home, which means it can offer speeds of up to 300 Mbps. Again, this is only available to certain addresses. There are a few new startup broadband companies with their own networks too, available to small parts of the UK, such as Gigaclear and Hyperoptic. Speed is one of the biggest selling points and therefore influencers on the price of broadband packages, but it is important not to hugely overpay – many do.

The law is changing, but at the moment internet service providers (ISPs) can advertise maximum amazing speeds with the use of the helpful words 'up to', even if only 10 per cent of customers can actually get them. So you might pay loads to get 76 Mbps, only to realize that because of your distance from the exchange, or the number of people on your street who want to watch *Walter Presents* at the same time, you will never get anywhere near that and you might as well have bought the budget, slower package that you are stuck paying for for the next twenty-four months. From 2019 you should be told the minimum average speeds you are likely to get for your address before you sign up to a deal.

By way of example, you need 3 Mbps of sustained bandwidth to watch iPlayer on high definition, according to *Which?* Netflix suggests a minimum of 5 Mbps to watch it in HD quality, and 25 Mbs for ultra-HD.

You need more if you regularly use broadband at the same time as other people in the house, for example if several flatmates watch Netflix at the same time, or you like to download films in a hurry (one film would take 23 minutes and 9 seconds to download with a 5 Mbps connection, and 1 minute 31 seconds with a 76 Mbps connection, says *Which?*). Unless ten of you are watching Netflix all day at once on different screens, 1 Gps (1,000 Mbps) could be wasted on your household.

When choosing broadband, beware of any exit fees for leaving your contract early, and any 'free' things thrown in, that may turn out to be far from free. A case I wrote about in *The Times* demonstrates how this can catch you out. In early 2018 BT was advertising a deal to existing BT broadband subscribers: add BT Sport on your contract free for six months, then for £10 a month from month seven. Great deal. Until the customer calls, and discovers that they have to sign up to a brand-new eighteen-month broadband contract to get BT Sport.

The customer was already paying £45.99 a month; the new deal would rise to £56.49 a month from 'month seven'. So BT Sport was indeed free for six months, but it would then cost the equivalent of £20.50 more (£10 plus the difference between his existing deal and the new one he had to sign up for), annulling the free period altogether. I wonder how many people did the maths, or just signed up because it sounded decent and ended up actually spending much more money with BT in the long run.

How to switch your broadband

First, once you've come to the end of your broadband contract you could call your existing provider and haggle to get a cheaper deal. Haggling works really well with broadband companies, and you can usually persuade them to match a deal you have found elsewhere. If like me you are far too British to haggle effectively on the phone, try using the online chat facility. Failing that, there are two ways to switch, with awful names: 'gaining provider led' and 'cease and reprovide'.

The first applies to anyone switching between ADSL broadband companies who has their line rental with BT, and it is easier. All you do is apply for your new deal, online, directly or through a comparison site, or on the phone. Your new provider will do the rest, cancel your old contract, and let you know when your new broadband is up and running. Cease and reprovide applies if you are switching away from ADSL to a company like Virgin Media, or vice versa. This is more manual; you need to call both companies and cancel your old deal and set up your new one, and try and match up the dates on which the old ends and new begins.

Ask your new provider for a speed estimate for your address and check whether you have to pay any connection fees or fees for a new router. **Note you have to give your old provider thirty days' notice to cancel your broadband (even once you are technically out of contract) to switch penalty-free.**

If you are planning to move home soon, check that your broadband provider will let you take

your connection with you or look for a short contract that rolls month by month. They will be more expensive but probably cheaper than paying massive penalty fees to exit early.

• •

Mobile phones

As with broadband, while most people sign up to long specified contracts – usually twenty-four months – no one will draw your attention when they end. This is set to change. Ofcom, the industry regulator, thinks it is unfair and has pledged to look into alerts to warn people.

You would be amazed how many people do not realize that it isn't happening yet. Mobile-phone companies are not under any obligation to monitor your usage either, so you could continue to pay £45 a month for a phone that you haven't touched for years. I've seen examples of people sold contract phones when they are in the early stages of dementia, who continue to get charged long after they have gone into residential homes, while the phone lies turned off in the back of a cupboard. These changes can amount to thousands of pounds.

You are not told because, naturally, most people forget, can't be bothered, and keep paying absolutely loads more than they need to. Mobile companies' excuse is that they do not want to inconvenience people by cutting off their phones out of the blue. This overpaying is especially steep when you have bought a contract that offers you a free or discounted smartphone, because you will be paying off the price of the phone long after you already 'own it' outright.

Estimates reckon that phone companies make £400 profit on the real cost of a handset like an iPhone over a typical two-year mobile-phone contract. That is £400 that could be lining your bank account. For that reason SIM-only deals are almost always better value. If you cannot afford to buy your phone up front with cash, you would usually be better off buying one on a 0 per cent interest credit card, and paying it down month by month, than you would taking out a contract with a 'free' phone and paying higher monthly phone-contract charges.

Many SIM-only deals also do not require you to sign up for a such a long contract. Some you can get for just one month, such as ID Mobile plans, which means you can switch it much faster and keep your eye out for the best-value deal, take a different one if you are on holiday for a month and need roaming in the USA, and so on.

The free-minutes and free-texts bundles are now all so generous that they can be ignored. (Remember the days when you would run out of texts!) It is all about the data. Data is where you get stung, too, for both underestimating and overestimating your usage.

While you can now use your phone in the EU as if you were at home, watch out if geography is not your strong point, when using it in European countries that are not in the EU (see Turkey). Phone companies do not always take a view on unreasonable bills. One poor man wrote to me to ask for help with his £18,500 phone bill, run up after he accidentally played some video advert that was downloading in the background of his phone all night – to a total of 6 Mb while he was on business in Moldova. Set a data cap on your bills, even if you never travel beyond the EU.

On the other hand, you do not want to pay unnecessarily for too much data as part of your contract. You can monitor your previous month's usage on your network's app, or use an online service like BillMonitor, invented by three mathematicians from Oxford University, where you can upload your bills, or use their online calculator to work out how much data you tend to use and what allowance you need.

Roughly speaking, watching a two-hour film on your phone in HD would use up 4.2 GB, streaming an hour of music 80 Mb, and downloading sixty web pages 140 Mb, according to uswitch.com, but social media autoplay videos are big culprits for munching through lots of data. The US company Wandera found that since the introduction of Stories, Instagram uses up 71.5 per cent more data; daily data usage on the app in 2017 was about 28.4 Mb per person. That amounts to 880.5 Mb a month, more than many affordable contracts offer.

Quick ways to cut your mobile data bill

There are easy ways to trim your unintentional data usage.

By default Instagram preloads videos. Adjust your settings in your Instagram profile by tapping mobile

data use and toggle on to 'use less data' to stop
this. Similarly stop autoplaying videos in Facebook
under the autoplay section in videos and photos
settings, and turn on data saver under the data-usage
autoplay settings in Twitter. If you use YouTube
change the settings so that videos play in HD only
when you have wifi access.

It is always better to download Spotify playlists to
your phone, but if you stream on the go, change
the quality to 'normal' rather than automatic.
If you have an iPhone, turn off wifi assist in
settings, a feature that switches your phone to data
automatically when your wifi connection is poor.

In settings toggle to off the slider of any apps that
you don't need when you're out and about – for
example, photos – which means your photos will
only back up to iCloud when you have wifi. Set
podcasts and Spotify to download only when you
are connected to wifi, too. Also turn off apps'
'background app refresh' settings. If you have an
Android you can set limits on data in settings and
a data-saver mode. You can also download apps
to keep tabs on data: Datally, for example, or
SmartApp.

Insurance

What you need and what you do not

You will probably use a comparison site to pick your insurance policy, but do so with caution and watch out for the reams of small print. Comparison sites often make crude assumptions about you to keep headline prices down, which if wrong can be costly. Each site has access to exclusive products and prices, which means that if you can be bothered it is worth collecting quotes from several, and also checking Aviva, Direct Line and Zurich, insurers that do not always appear on comparison sites.

With most insurance policies you will have to pay an excess when you make a claim. This is a sum of cash you will have to pay up front. Higher excesses result in lower premiums and vice versa, but not always. Insurers normally give a premium discount for higher excesses, but sometimes the discount can be quite small compared with the premium saving. It might be worth paying a few pounds more on the premium if it means receiving hundreds of pounds more if you make a big claim.

Here's what you need, and what you do not.

Home insurance

There are two types of home insurance to consider: buildings and contents.

If you have a mortgage then you are obliged to have buildings cover by law. If you rent then you don't need to worry about it, your landlord will sort it. Buildings cover protects the physical building – walls, roof, windows, fitted kitchen and bathroom – from damage as a result of fire, flood, subsidence and so on.

Contents insurance is optional, and covers the stuff inside your house from similar accidents or theft.

• BUILDINGS INSURANCE

You need to choose a policy that has a big enough 'sum insured' to completely rebuild your home should some disaster happen. This is not the same as the value of your home: it will be less. You don't want to be under-insured, but equally there is no point in being over-insured and paying too much. Insurers offer unlimited costs so you do not have to do the maths, but that could mean you end up with something pricier than necessary. You can figure out how much it would cost to rebuild your property using the Building Cost Information Service online calculator on the Association of British Insurers' website.

Review your buildings insurance every so often, because rebuild costs do rise over the years, though some insurers offer policies that increase the sum insured automatically. Be sure to review if you do major building works, or add an extension that may mean that your property will cost more to rebuild.

Your mortgage provider may try to sell you buildings insurance, but you have zero obligation to go with them. This is a common assumption, though. I had a letter from a reader who had been paying five times more than necessary to insure her home because she had stuck with the same insurer that her mortgage provider suggested.

• CONTENTS INSURANCE

Decide if you want contents insurance based on whether or not you want to take the risk of losing any possessions should your home get broken into, or there is a fire or flood. The average contents insurance policy cost £139 a year in 2017 for the average home, which contains £35,000 worth of removable stuff according to the Association of British Insurers. You may also be able to get cover for accidental damage – for example spilling a bottle of red wine on your sofa – but this is not always automatically included. Check if you want it.

Again you need to work out the value of everything you might want replacing in your home, from clothes to knives and forks. You could save the hassle and get a policy with unlimited cover, or a bedroom rating where the insurer assesses how much your possessions are worth based on how many bedrooms you have. **You really do not want to under-insure, whatever you decide. Here is a useful example from the Money Advice Service. Say that all your possessions are worth £40,000 but you only insure them for £20,000. You are burgled and lose your TV, sound system and two laptops worth a total of £5,000, and you make a claim on your contents insurance. Because your total contents insurance cover is half what it should have been, your insurer could actually reduce your claim payment by half too, so you would only receive £2,500 for the items.**

Most important with insuring the stuff in your home from damage or theft is to check upper limits on individual items. Many policies have a maximum 'single-item limit', often £1,500, which could mean that an engagement ring or fancy camera may fall outside the standard policy.

If you want to take items insured outside the home you will probably need to pay extra for 'personal possessions cover' to protect you if your laptop or bike gets nicked. Note that this could help keep travel insurance down, too, because some policies cover your personal possessions abroad. Check so that you are not doubling up and spending more money than you need to.

Look out too for whether you are paying 'new for old', which is where you get a payout of what it actually costs to replace whatever you might lose, or indemnity cover, where you only get the current value of your possessions. The latter will be cheaper but could work out as false economy.

Often insurers will set certain security conditions, such as having approved locks and alarms fitted to your home. If your insurer specifies these, you must do what they say and use them, otherwise your claim could be rejected and there was no point in paying for insurance in the first place.

Mobile and gadget insurance

If you are someone forever losing their top-of-the-range smartphone, then you might want to consider mobile insurance, though pick wisely, because it can be very expensive – several hundred pounds a year. Look for policies that start at around £5 or £6 a month. Mobile-phone insurance offered by networks is usually priciest.

If you get personal-possession cover as part of your home insurance then it will cover phones and gadgets. The downside of this is that the excess may be higher, cancelling out the benefit somewhat, though if you have a new iPhone it will probably be worth it. You may have to wait longer to get your phone repaired or replaced under your home insurance too. You may also lose a no-claims discount on your home insurance if you claim for a lost phone, which will up the cost of your whole contents insurance policy for the next few years.

Mobile and gadget insurance can, however, tend not to pay out when you might assume it would. Watch out for policies that do not cover water damage, or are strict about you taking 'reasonable care', which means they would not cover you if you did something dumb and left your phone in an airplane pocket, for example, as I did once. Some only cover you for stolen phones, not for lost ones. Most insurers will not cover you unless you report your phone stolen or lost immediately, at least within the first twelve hours; some offer a more generous twenty-four-hour window.

Find out whether you will get a repair or refurbished phone, rather than a replacement or the cash payout. It varies.

Car insurance

If you have a car it must be insured, so there's no question of whether or not you need this cover. Unfortunately, it is really expensive. The average car-insurance bill is now £752 a year, according to insurer Willis Towers Watson. Automatic renewal is particularly bad news with car insurance, too: you could end up paying an unbelievable amount more than you need to. **Gocompare found a £1,635 difference in premium for the same cover:**

a 27-year-old living in north London driving a 2016 Ford Fiesta would pay £361 with Admiral and £1,996 with Wise Driving. So if there's one insurance you are going to put the time into shopping around for each year, this is the one. Think how many hours you have to work to earn £1,635.

Your level of risk, which is what will determine the price of your car insurance, is based on various obscure factors. Early this year it was revealed that, hilariously, motorists pay £31 more if they have a hotmail email address rather than a gmail address. Certain domain names (let's be honest, you probably have an opinion of someone who still uses BT Openworld) are associated with greater risk of car accidents or fraudulent claims.

Also how you define your occupation matters. You could save £35.43 by defining yourself as a teacher rather than a music teacher, according to one comparison site. You should also always state if you are retired or a stay-at-home parent, rather than calling yourself unemployed – it could save you £139.69. You should also time when you buy insurance. Prices are most expensive on the day your existing policy is set to expire. Apparently the cheapest time to buy is three weeks before that, which could save you several hundred pounds. I have also been told that you should not apply for car insurance in the middle of the night: I guess it makes you look less reliable? Or more tired?

Check what is included in your car-insurance quote: there could be all sorts you do not need, such as driving abroad, or things you are already paying for, such as theft from the car, which may be already covered by home or mobile-phone insurance. You might not need extra breakdown cover if you are already a member of the AA. You will be able to pay for your car insurance in two ways, monthly or as a lump sum. Avoid the monthly option, *Which?* estimates it will cost you £100 more.

If you are a young, relatively new but sensible driver, consider black box car insurance, or telematics. This is a box fitted to your car to monitor how you drive and prove that you are not too risky, which should bring your cover down from the high average usually applied to younger people. You might also want to take the Pass Plus driving course, which may reduce your cover with some insurers.

Travel insurance

One of the worst cases I have ever dealt with at *The Times* involved a reader who, on holiday with his family in Florida, was injured in a hit and run and had to be airlifted to hospital. He was treated over three weeks for broken bones in his feet, legs and chest, and the bill came to $150,000. He had travel insurance, but because when he was hit by the car he had been walking home from dinner, during which he had drunk alcohol, his insurer refused to pay. He was facing having to sell his home to clear the bill.

Eventually, after the story was published, the insurer relented and paid out, agreeing that there was no causal link between the accident and the beer, but it was a lesson in, first, how expensive it can be if you do not have travel insurance on holiday, and second, how insurers will try to wriggle out of paying even seemingly cut-and-dried claims.

You should not always opt for the cheapest travel insurance you can find. Consider what might lurk in the small print. One insurance-industry insider told me he would always buy travel insurance from a big-brand company because they will not want the reputational damage of refusing a

massive claim for someone who falls ill, whereas some little fly-by-night company that can quickly change its name may be less reliable when it comes to meeting an obligation.

Most important is to find enough medical cover when choosing travel insurance. The rest matters less. Go for one that covers you for at least £2 million of medical expenses in Europe and £5 million worldwide, according to Dr Matthew Connell, director of policy at the Chartered Insurance Institute, which will cover you for a flight home by air ambulance if necessary. Who knows what will happen after Brexit, but at the moment, in the EU you are entitled to free state medical care with the European Health Insurance Card (EHIC). You can rely on this instead of medical insurance, but you need to make sure you are not treated as a private patient but in the public health system. There have been instances where people are automatically treated privately, costing them thousands.

Other things you might want as part of your travel insurance include about £3,000 of cancellation or curtailment cover, if something stops you going on your holiday, and £1,500 for loss or theft of your bags or possessions, though it is up to you whether you are fussed about this. As I mention above, some home-insurance policies will cover you. Check whether you get any cover for lost or delayed baggage. If your bag is lost it is much quicker and more lucrative to claim compensation on your insurance than via an airline.

Common exclusions to keep in mind include insurance being invalidated if you drink or take drugs (see the case above), if you have to cancel your holiday because you are pregnant or because a relative dies as a result of an existing condition that you already knew about, or if a relative or friend dies and they are not deemed 'close enough' to you.

If you have any pre-existing health conditions or have had something like cancer in the past, you need to search a bit harder for good-value cover. Try the British Insurance Brokers Association (biba.org.uk), who can direct you to insurers that cover particular illnesses. If you are going skiing or diving you will need a specialist add-on or policy.

Travel insurance is either for a single trip or annual. The latter usually works out better value if you go on two or more holidays in a year.

The average multi-trip annual policy costs £50, according to moneysupermarket.com. Most annual policies will have a limit on the length of the trip, usually about thirty-one days, so if you are going travelling or on a sabbatical, you will need something more tailored.

Critical illness, mortgage protection and life insurance

Have you ever considered what you would do if you were too ill to work, and therefore to pay your rent or the mortgage? Or if you died suddenly, how your family would pay the rent or the mortgage? Or what would happen if you lost your job? Income-protection insurance is designed to pay out if you are unemployed, fall ill, or get injured so that you cannot work. Life insurance pays out a sum of money, or an income, to your relatives if you die. Give some thought to whether you need it.

Many jobs pay decent redundancy or sick pay, and you get government benefits if you fall ill or cannot work. There are also benefits to cover your mortgage-interest payments, and you may be able to negotiate a pause on your mortgage with your bank while you try to get back on your feet. Perhaps you have relatives that could put you up should something awful happen to you or your partner. However, if you are self-employed, or if you have children or other dependants, few savings, and if moving house when you cannot work in the same job is unthinkable, then it is an important safety net.

Some income protection is much, much better than others. In another sad reader case, one self-employed 32-year-old man was sold a cheapo income-protection policy which refused to pay out when he was in hospital having seizures and a blood transfusion because it did not deem him 'ill enough'. This policy was based not on his inability to do his job – you want to look for this type known as 'own occupation' – but his inability to do a set number of tasks or 'activities of daily living', which the insurer rated as criteria for whether or not he could work. This included ridiculously basic things that you could do from your hospital bed, like hold a pen and lift a 1kg weight.

The same is true of what is known as critical illness. These are insurance policies that pay out a large sum of money if you have a serious condition that meets your insurer's criteria – things like cancer, stroke, heart attack or organ transplant. Frustratingly, these policies often do not pay out for the most likely causes of your being unable to work for a long period, things like chronic back pain or mental-health problems. A good-quality own-occupation income-protection policy should cover you for any health problem that means you cannot do your own job.

Your mortgage broker or bank may try to sell you income protection when you take out a loan. Do not just opt for what they offer. They are more likely to try to sell you life insurance with critical illness, rather than the more complicated but more comprehensive income protection, and often a policy that will only cover your mortgage, rather than something that is more far-reaching, which you may also require in order to cover bills or daily costs if you fall ill.

If you are single and renting, or a young couple with no significant commitments, then it is probably not necessary to have a policy that pays out a sum of money if you should die. But as above, if you have children, or a mortgage with someone else who would be unable to deal with your household expenses alone should you pass away, then it is definitely worth buying.

As Tom Connor, director of Drewberry insurance specialists, points out to me, it may be really hard for a surviving parent to go back to work at all if their partner dies and they have a child to care for. If you were both to die in a freak accident, your children would benefit from a financial payout. Life insurance would pay off your mortgage in both instances. Connor recommends a family-income-benefit policy which pays an annual income to a remaining partner with a policy term to run until your youngest child is twenty-one. If you think you need income protection or life insurance it is wise to speak to an independent financial adviser to make sure you buy something that will genuinely protect you and your family, because they are not straightforward products, and it is a waste of money, as well as risky, to buy something substandard.

PART TWO

Introduction: how does money make you feel?

By this stage you should have a clearer idea of whether or not you can buy a house, save and budget better, start a pension, claim back any tax or invest for your future. But being smart about money, and, more importantly, feeling good about money, is about more than implementing clever personal finance tricks. I have written this book, I know that credit cards are expensive and I should save more in a pension, but still I get caught out. Why?

In the next two chapters I look at how money can make us feel, how it can impact on our happiness in relationships, our sense of self-worth and ultimately our mental health. I offer some practical guidance on how to tackle money, the trickiest of subjects, with your partner, your family, and ultimately, yourself.

10
Money
and love

Here is a money dilemma for you:

> I'm moving in with my boyfriend who owns
> his own flat, and he has suggested that I pay
> him rent. We will then split the bills fifty-fifty.
> My friends have said that he is profiting from
> me because my money will go towards paying
> off his mortgage. He owns a one-bedroom flat,
> so it's not like he was going to rent a room to
> another person. I can't afford to buy into his
> place as I have no savings, and I think it's a bit
> soon for that level of commitment anyway.
> Should I object and ask to pay less? Obviously
> this is a bit of a tricky topic to bring up.

What do you think? Is he out of order? Is she out of
order for even thinking twice about paying rent? Are
her friends out of order for sharing their unsettling
opinions? Is anyone out of order here? Help!

Unfortunately there is no 'turn to page 57' for the
correct answer. Try bringing it up with a mixed
group, pour yourself a glass of wine, sit back and
watch the fallout as everyone thinks what she should
do is obvious.

I lifted this dilemma from the *Telegraph*'s Moral
Money section, but it is nowadays an extremely

and increasingly common one as people cohabit and partner up at different stages of life, often out of necessity and therefore slightly sooner than is comfortable. Living together is much cheaper than living apart, and for a growing number living alone is a financial impossibility.

This is a dilemma that is further complicated when people have bought properties with loans or gifts from wary parents. A recent, awful, survey by NFU Mutual – I am not sure it is totally scientific – suggests that a fifth of the Bank of Mum and Dad cite their children's partners as 'money-grabbing, secretive, dishonest and lacking in intelligence', a quarter said they would like their son- or daughter-in-law to be excluded from benefiting from any gifts or inheritance altogether. Gritty teeth emoji to the family Whatsapp group.

Despite the prevalence of this modern arrangement, people are so loaded up with emotional responses to money, gendered expectations, different senses of duty and what amounts to good manners, that they really do not see eye to eye about how couples should divide up their finances or their property. The result is a lot of hurt and passive-aggressive receipt filing. Nor is this helped by the fact that we

Brits find money an awkward topic of discussion, so how everyone else sorts it out remains a bit of a mystery.

I could tell you all of my friends' online dating stories: the really fit Orlando Bloom lookalike who kept nipping out of the bedroom to open the door of his flat (to sell cocaine, it later transpired); another who insisted on wearing my friend's knickers. We have shared our intimate health conditions, the ins and outs of our imposter-syndrome fears, the times one shoplifted bindis from Claire's Accessories or another cried because she did not really enjoy the fuss of her wedding day.

Yet – and perhaps it is strange that I have never asked, as they would probably tell me – I do not know how much any of my closest friends earn, whether their partners earn more or less, or how much, if any, debt they have on their credit cards. With a few exceptions, I have no idea when most of my friends stopped getting handouts from their parents too, or whether they ever did. Did they buy their flat because they stopped buying flat whites or because someone helped?

This is another classic source of modern money stress: are you not able to afford your own place because you are not working as hard, or saving as hard as your acquaintances, or do they have a secret income they have not told you about? My friends and I, we Brits in general, do not talk as easily and freely about money as we might other formerly taboo topics like, er, sleeping with drug dealers, or IBS.

And it seems that the same goes for other nations. In the first episode of the US podcast 'Bad with money', comedian Gaby Dunn approaches some young people in a coffee shop in LA and asks them what their favourite sexual position is. Without much hesitation one says 'Reverse cowgirl.' Gaby then asks how much money is in her bank account, and she says: 'Wow, yeah, I don't want to answer that one!' Too personal.

And so to the anonymous comments section of the *Telegraph* where people have free rein to unleash what they really feel about love and money without fear of judgement. The number of comments suggests that this is a popular pastime. An online survey underneath the dilemma asked how many people think yes, the reader should pay rent, or no, she shouldn't. Of the 2,300 who voted, 55 per cent said yes and 45 per cent no. Not a vast difference.

Meanwhile the hundreds of comments range from 'Don't move in until you buy a place TOGETHER'; 'If her boyfriend becomes her unofficial landlord they are doomed'; and 'If he owns the property I think it's insane that you should pay rent and not have a stake in it', to 'Does seem a lot of women want it all for free'; 'Reminds me of a line from the madame in the brothel in *Westworld* . . . Maeve: You're always paying for it darling. The difference is our costs are fixed and posted right there on the door', and then: 'NO WAY ! NO, NO, NO DON'T DO THIS!'

So that clears it up.

Back when my grandma and grandad moved in together they were, as was the way, married, and very young. She gave up work outside the home, and he provided for her through his paid job, then private pension, for ever; that was for most of that era an expected and largely unquestioned arrangement. My grandma was engaged with the household finances, but many women in the 1950s had no idea what their husbands earned. Amazingly to me, many still do not: according to a recent study by Prudential one in five have no idea of their partner's salary.

The automatic male-sole-breadwinner arrangement, with the woman receiving an allowance for housekeeping, persisted well into the 1980s and 1990s, too. Until the late Seventies, when my (married) mum and dad bought their first flat together, women were routinely rejected for a mortgage unless they had a male guarantor.

The Tinder generation is the first to enjoy the blissful freedom of no apparent rules or expectations about who earns and who pays, and yet I still roll my eyes at the TV when, of the heterosexual couples, men are always expected to get their cards out on (one of my fave TV shows) *First Dates* and the women demur just the polite amount. Or someone posts a picture of their gigantic sparkling engagement ring from their bae. There is always a survey that investigates whether or not relationships where the woman earns more cause men and women to have worse sex. Meanwhile, companies fail to pay men taking shared parental leave as much as they would their female employees taking maternity, or accept that men should be entitled to as much time off without damaging their careers.

My own anecdotal research suggests many happy couples often harbour secret resentments over their finances, too. One tells me that the finances in her and her boyfriend's relationship have always been pretty imbalanced, as he is self-employed and she earns a higher regular wage. 'I don't believe that equality goes pound for pound, I believe that we will both make different contributions at different points in our lives that will help us to explore different opportunities,' she wrote to me in an email.

But it is frustrating to be the one who pays for all the food shops and trips away. I know if the tables were turned then he would do the same. But that doesn't mean it doesn't get annoying. I will sometimes more keenly and slightly begrudgingly notice if he's spent a chunk of money on something I don't value as much as he does, even if I go out and buy a ridiculous scented candle from Anthropologie. In my head, for a split second I think 'well I worked hard for money to spunk on a candle, but he's not working as hard and doesn't earn enough to pay for food, so why is he buying that?'

The feeling normally passes, but it adds a strain. Similarly, he has moments when he admits that not being able to contribute as much financially gets him down, he feels like he's not able to

build the life he wants to with me and feels a
bit 'less'.

Nobody offers you a handbook about how modern
couples should talk about or manage their money,
or any real insight into what other people do.
Perhaps not uncoincidentally, then, money is the
prime source of tension between couples who wind
up at relationship-counselling organization Relate.

'Money represents power, and that's why the
dynamic is such a strong one,' says Peter Saddington,
a Relate relationship and family counsellor, who says
money is a fairly constant theme that he sees coming
up with clients. 'Whether that is power between a
couple or between a parent and a child, who has
money and who hasn't got it, and how it gets spent.
Often in couple relationships money starts coming
up fairly early on – you are dating, who pays for
what? If issues start arising at that point and they do
not get dealt with it is like a ticking time bomb that
will go off at a later stage.'

A common sticking point is when a couple first have
a child. Money becomes much more of an issue,
there is less around, who is bringing it in? Power
dynamics can come to a head. Peter says that if they

haven't talked about it beforehand a couple can be in crisis. Assumptions are made – 'I thought this, I didn't think he'd say this.' They have not actually talked about the nitty-gritty.

Cate Campbell, relationship therapist and member of the British Association for Counselling and Psychotherapy, agrees. 'Where there is conflict, money management or lack of it almost always comes up as a source of distress. It is very present for almost all couples at some point, for some, a constant source of friction.'

Many partners feel that the other's financial behaviour affects their own self-image. They may have unrealistic ideas about what's possible, especially if they grew up in a financially very secure or very insecure household. 'There's a lot of shame around money and status. What one partner sees as evidence of success the other may just view as unacceptable showing off or wasteful,' says Cate. 'This may prevent couples from talking about money because it can lead to arguments and tension or just bring up issues that can't be resolved and cause stress.'

For some couples, money worries are shared and, although this creates pressure on the relationship, they see it as an external stress. It is a much bigger problem if couples blame each other for overspending or not earning enough. Common issues that Cate sees include how to spend money and what on, how to deal with unexpected windfalls, bonuses or inheritances, who do they belong to? How money is spent on other family members such as children or parents, or when one half of a couple is being financially secretive, or dipping into savings.

'Talking about money can cause a lot of stress and some counselling sessions turn out to just be about mediating how and when finances will be talked about,' she adds. 'Generally, couples don't discuss or plan nearly enough around their finances, or anything else, before they marry or move in together.'

How to discuss money with your loved ones

'In Western culture, we don't talk about money easily. This can be overcome by realizing you can talk about it, and the world doesn't end when you do,' says Peter, whose advice is, as unromantic and awkward as it might be, to address the topic head on as soon as you can as a young couple – 'It is not one of those topics to save until later on if you can help it.'

Resentments can at first be small and petty, but if they do not get dealt with they become big insurmountable things, which counsellors say can be the reason why people get into much more aggressive and destructive arguments.

First get your head around your own subconscious attitudes and expectations around money. Examine what influences how you think about money and your values towards money, some of which may have been instilled as a child, and the role it may play in your relationship. If you understand what is influencing you, it is not the influence you want, and it is unconsciously affecting you, you can change it.

If you want to discuss how you will manage money together, have a conversation about the money conversation you are going to have, and when. Plan it to take the heat out of it. How are you going to make it a safe topic? It can feel like a threat, with one or the other being judged. That might not be the intent, but there can be a difference in how you perceive it and what you've grown up with.

For most couples Cate says a weekly or monthly catch-up is helpful, but keep points brief, outlining the problem and how you suggest it might be managed. The ideal conversation should only last twenty minutes. Try not to let it spiral. If you are going to make a big financial commitment – a car, a house – ask each other: When we buy this, is it mine? Is it ours? What is going to be each person's involvement?

Contracting is often used in the counselling room to take the pressure out of a money discussion. Writing down and talking about what you want to go in the contract before any agreement is made can be useful. You might agree that you each have a pot of money that you can say is your own, not 'ours', and I can choose to spend it as I wish, and you are not allowed to comment on this. I can give it all to my children, or spend it on a coat, or buy a present for you. Then you might have a pot of money assigned for joint spending, and work out what your budget should be for this. Perhaps it is 50:50, or the person who earns more puts money in. Draw up an agreement about what you feel is fair and stick to it.

Consider a third pot for joint savings, agree what will go in it and what you are going to spend it on, and when you can access it. You could put in place 'spending limits', where anything above that sum requires a joint decision before you buy it. And try to make sure you are both fully understanding of finances, how much each other earns, and what bills you have to pay.

If one person earns lots more than the other, or one of you is not earning – because they are staying at home to look after children, for example – discuss whether you want to have an allowance system, or a way that the non-earner receives money into their personal bank account, or a joint account. If so make it clear that this is not a gift or favour.

Should you get a joint account?

The humble joint account, a current account that you take out with another person, or multiple people, giving you all a debit-card and access to manage it, is not as benign as it sounds. Think carefully and talk about the pros and cons together before you open one. While you probably do not want to be combing through each other's credit histories on date number two, try to get to the bottom of whether your other half has had any money troubles, payday loans or substantial debts in the last six years or so before you sign up to link your finances.

Your credit score is not impacted by just living with someone, but once you have opened a joint account your credit histories are linked, so your score could be ruined by a partner's bad habits, making it harder for you to get a loan, mobile-phone contract or mortgage.

A joint account also leaves you both 'jointly and severally liable', which means that you are both responsible for what is in the account, and to pay, for example, any overdraft charges. It also means that if one of you refuses to do so, the other still has to cover it. If your fellow joint-account holder disappears into the sunset, having emptied the account and run up a massive overdraft, a bank can pursue you for the debt, even if you were unaware of it.

Some banks let one person close a joint account, but others require both or all parties to sign and send off a form to close it, or for a couple to visit a branch together. This can be really difficult if you have split up and are on bad terms, or, as one *Times* reader wrote to me, if your partner is controlling. She was unable to close her joint account without her partner's consent. He refused but continued to run up debts which she had to clear. If you are in any doubt speak to the bank about what would happen if you wanted to close the account without the other account holder present.

You cannot get a joint credit card, but you can have an additional cardholder added to your account. This means that you are liable for any spending they make, but you can also close it at any time. If you are not ready to take the plunge you could use a prepaid card, which, like a pay-as-you-go mobile, you could both top up with a set budget for joint household spending, without the fear of accruing debts. Most are offered by Mastercard or Visa, so can be used anywhere that accepts normal Mastercard or Visa debit and credit cards – see Pockit, FairFX, Optimum, Post Office.

They also do not require a credit check, so will not affect your credit score. You can add an additional cardholder with a prepaid card so that both of you have a card for spending. The downside is that prepaid cards are subject to lots of hidden fees, so gen up on what they are. You might pay a one-off application fee to open it, or a monthly fee to use it, or a percentage fee for transactions, or a fee if you do not spend a set amount.

When I first started living with my other half, before we reached the great joint-account watermark in our relationship, we would individually spend on joint things then save receipts. We could never, ever be bothered to go through them, but every six months or so we'd reach a tipping point at which we had to sit down and tackle the mountain of paper that was starting to take up expensive London real-estate square footage. Now there are apps that can do it for you, such as Receipts by Wave. The new breed of online-only app banks – see Monzo, Starling and Revolut – let you take photos of your receipts and tag spending. You could add a note that your Costcutters shop was for joint household essentials, or easily split a bill with friends and family who will receive funds into their account instantly.

Cohabiting: your rights, or lack thereof

There are many pub lawyers out there expounding myths about 'common-law marriage'. Resolution, the family law organization, says that two-thirds of cohabiting couples are unaware that common-law marriage is not actually a fact: it has no legal grounding in the UK. There is work going on to change this, but slow progress is being made. **If you are living together but are not married or in a civil partnership, you have few automatic rights and can be in a very vulnerable position if your relationship ends. If you are married or in a civil partnership there is a legal obligation for you to be financially supported by your ex-spouse. Not so if you are just living together, even if you have been living together for decades.**

There is a big debate under way about whether this is fair while 3.3 million families cohabit, according to a Families and Household survey by the Office of National Statistics in 2017, and the cohabiting family type is the fastest-growing of any family structure, more than doubling since 1996 when just 1.5 million families cohabited.

'Unlike a marriage, where a spouse can ask the court to order provision from their partner [if they split up], a cohabitee may have to move out of the family home with no right to return or receive any payment towards rehousing themselves,' says Bryan Scant, a family solicitor for Coffin Mew. 'There is scope in the law to help people in those situations, but it is not as straightforward as divorce and often costlier. It is vital that until the government reviews this law, couples are made aware of the risky position that they may find themselves in by not being married, and take steps, with appropriate legal advice, to protect themselves.'

Paula Myers, national head of will, trust and estate disputes at law firm Irwin Mitchell Private Wealth, says that without any sort of agreement in place, or updated will, couples could spend their entire adult lives together and still be literally left out in the cold once their partner dies because they have limited claim to any of their money.

Cohabiters can also struggle to get life-insurance payouts and pension entitlements if their partners die, which are automatically paid out to widows and widowers. 'Some can struggle to access bank accounts or even have a say on how a funeral is arranged,' says Ms Myers, who cites 'common issues' she has seen as people having to sue their own under-sixteen-year-old children to get access to money to pay the mortgage of the home they shared with their long-term unmarried partner. She says she expects to see more problems involving cohabitees: 'While the law remains non-existent for cohabiting couples there will be disputes down the line.'

If you are renting with a partner but you are not married you are most probably both on the tenancy agreement, in which case you are 'jointly and severally liable' for the rent and for any damage made to your rental property. If you move in with a partner who is renting and just pay them rent, however, you have no rights over the property and can be booted out by the landlord or indeed a disgruntled ex.

It is more complicated when it comes to property ownership. Here are a few scenarios, how to manage them, and what they might mean for you.

• YOU LIVE IN YOUR PARTNER'S PROPERTY BUT ARE NOT ON THE MORTGAGE, OR YOU OWN A PROPERTY AND YOUR BOYFRIEND OR GIRLFRIEND MOVES IN WITHOUT BEING ADDED TO THE MORTGAGE

If, like our *Telegraph* reader friend at the start of this chapter, you move in with your boyfriend or girlfriend who owns their own property, you are most exposed. You have no automatic right to own any part of it should you split up, even if you had been paying them money that they put towards the mortgage, for decades, and even if you have children. You may be able to argue that your ex-partner should pay maintenance for your child, which could include providing a home for them in which you could live, but you would not own that home and would have to leave it when the children are independent.

There is, however, a law called the Trusts of Land and Appointment of Trustees Act 1996 ('TOLATA'), that allows people to take legal action against a former partner for a stake in a property if they can argue they have made a contribution and become a 'beneficial owner', even though their name is not on the deeds as a legal owner. Lawyer Andrew Leakey, head of dispute resolution and probate at

Stephenson's solicitors, says he deals with these claims regularly, but they can be expensive and messy cases, best avoided.

The key to claiming that you are entitled to part of the value of the home is to prove that you as a couple had a joint intention and agreement that you would contribute financially – for example by informally paying down the mortgage, or if you bankrolled an extension, or paid some cash into the deposit. This is not easy, however, because you need to produce evidence. The best piece of evidence is a declaration of trust, or a cohabitation agreement, a kind of prenup for the unmarried. **A declaration of trust is a legal document. You draw one up with a solicitor and pay about £150 to £450, setting out how you would divide up the value of your property should you split up.**

If this is too heavy-handed for where you are at in your relationship, and you prefer not to make it legal but would like to structure a discussion about where you may stand in the future should the worst happen, you might want to consider a more informal living-together agreement. This is a written promise between you and your partner

about what you both own and how you want to share it, including house as well as savings, possessions or debts. You can download the forms or advice on how to put one together, and what to include, on the website advicenow.org.uk.

I know from experience that deciding how best to split housing costs if one of you has much more money than the other can involve many toe-curling discussions far too early on.

I'd already fallen quite hard for the newish man in my life, with his chiselled cheekbones and exotic Swedish name (actual hometown: seaside Essex), when, at the age of twenty-five, he inherited some money. My boyfriend was ten years old when his dad passed away from cancer. Before he died, his dad left in trust some money for my boyfriend to spend once he was old enough to do something sensible with it. Most sensible was to use it, as soon as possible, towards a deposit on a flat to live in, but we had already rented together for a year. Given the cost of London, living together saved us both too much cash to ignore, plus we loved cohabiting. Where did that leave us? Would I be sleeping with my landlord?

In the end we decided that, given that my earthly possessions consisted of some Zara dresses, some badly framed posters and a significant overdraft, my boyfriend would own the flat and be responsible for all repairs, renovations and buildings insurance, and we would split all the bills except the mortgage 50:50. Rather than paying him rent, which felt too transactional and would have meant he benefited much more from the arrangement than I did, I saved the equivalent of his mortgage repayments into an untouchable savings account.

We reviewed it every so often to check whether or not I was missing out on owning a property myself, but nope, I still would not have been able to afford to buy in London had I been renting elsewhere. The promise was that I was investing for our future and he would benefit from our savings too should we stay together. Should we split up we both would have something to show for it. We made a decent bet that things would work out. Last year, after ten years together, we got married, and with the savings, and the rather more significant sum he had made by selling 'our' former flat (or 'his', I'm still not totally sure), bought our first joint home, in both our names.

It is not straight-down-the-middle fair, he will always have brought more to the table, but it is a rare and lucky couple that are both in exactly the same financial position when they meet, and stay that way as they grow old. Who knows what the future holds. Perhaps one day I'll make my fortune and more than pay him back.

• COHABITING BUT BOTH ON THE MORTGAGE

If you are unmarried but buying a home together and combining more or less the same amount of money each, then you can both go on the mortgage and deeds as legal owners, or what is known as 'joint tenants'. This means you own the property 50:50 but are both legally and independently liable for mortgage payments, whoever is actually living in the property and whether or not the other pays. If your boyfriend or girlfriend stops paying the mortgage, the bank can chase you for the debt in full. If you split up you will both have to work out what to do with the property, but you are entitled to half the proceeds from sale, or to be 'bought out' – where one stays and one moves out and the staying ex-partner pays for the other's share of the property.

If one of you is bringing more money than the other you may decide to own a property as tenants in common. This is where you both have an interest but one party's may be greater than the other. You can split it as you wish – maybe 60:40 or 80:20. You should draw up a declaration of trust with a solicitor to set this out. You will receive the appropriate percentage of proceeds from the property if it's sold.

• WHAT HAPPENS IF ONE OF YOU DIES?

If you are joint tenants then legally the property passes over to full ownership of the surviving cohabitee. If you are tenants in common, however, this is not the case. If you do not have a will the share of the property that your partner owned will pass instead automatically to their next of kin, either their children, or parents, or siblings.

If your partner draws up a will and leaves their share of the property to you, you may still be liable for inheritance tax. You pay 40 per cent inheritance tax on any sum of money above the threshold, which is £325,000. You may be able to bring a legal claim to inherit your partner's property in full if you are tenants in common and you have lived together for at least two years before death, whether or not they left a will. This can be a long and expensive process, however; far better that you draw up a will now.

There are several ways of drawing up a will. You can put one together yourself, a DIY will, but beware: if there is a mistake it is invalidated. Solicitors will charge about £150 upwards for something guaranteed. Will-writing firms can be cheaper, but they are unregulated and can be dodgy, so I would avoid them, especially if you are talked into them overseeing probate or executing your will themselves.

Every November Will Aid provides basic wills from hundreds of solicitors, and there is no minimum age. Ideally you donate about £95 to charity to have your will written up. You can also get a will drawn up with a solicitor by some charities free, in return for a donation to the charity. Also check out *Which?* or Co-op Legal.

Many private pension schemes provide a 'spouse pension' on death, whereby a portion of the pension pot is paid to the widow or widower, but this does not automatically apply to cohabitees, so if you are concerned you should look into the Ts & Cs of your pension policy. The same goes for life-insurance payouts that may be part of your job contract.

Any non-joint bank accounts or savings pots or possessions such as cars, laptops, jewellery or record collections will not go to you as a cohabitee on death unless you specifically state that they should in a will, however long you have lived together. Cohabitees also do not qualify for government bereavement benefits, such as widowed parent's allowance, if their partner dies. This has been heavily criticized for harming bereaved children who have no say over whether or not their parents are married. Let's hope the law will change soon.

11
Money
and
wellbeing

You have no doubt come across the concept of self-care, probably in relation to cutting down your booze consumption, working on your sleep hygiene, downloading a mindfulness app then trying not to look at your phone too much. I propose that you add, as a priority: Be kinder to yourself about money. There are few more emotive, yet oddly taboo topics. We should not be afraid to admit how bad money can make us feel.

Sadly, the shame and insecurity surrounding being honest about money worries and money fuckups makes them even more likely to make us feel awful, a problem shared is a problem halved and all. The jury's out on whether money can buy you happiness, but there is no doubt that not having a sense that you are in control of it, or believing, whatever your income, that you are not earning enough of it, can have a negative impact on your wellbeing.

Maybe you cannot afford a comfortable place to live, cannot afford to pay off your credit cards or gambling debts, do not seem valued enough for a pay rise at work, or simply consider yourself worse off compared with your peers – unable to afford the lifestyle that they lead or the restaurants that they book. Or, perhaps, like my friend and fellow money journalist Leah, whose bipolar disorder cost her £25,000 in eight months, you are struggling with a mental-health condition that has symptoms of manic overspending, or depression and anxiety that makes you unable to open a letter from your bank or make a phone call to your energy company – both extremely common. I offer some practical tips with how to deal with this situation further in this chapter.

A quarter of people will experience a mental-health issue this year, but we are all liable to let money, and the emotions surrounding it, get on top of us, to hold our nose and get a credit card out in a social situation that we cannot really afford, to comfort-shop on a rainy day.

The top point of comparison in an obviously flippant but telling enough *GQ* feature headlined 'Are you better than the average man?', based on most popular internet searches, is average income, the number-one yardstick of alpha status. Higher up the list than – shocker – average penis size, average height and average IQ.

Meanwhile, we are told that what we buy no longer defines us as it once did, ostentatious materialism is naff, and even the boss of Ikea says we've reached 'peak stuff'. But I am not convinced. All those authentic, social-media-documented 'experiences', insta interiors, travel and food porn invariably require cash. I often wonder how those part-time bloggers/curators earn so much, but they probably don't: they get their enviable lives subsidized by tourist boards or fashion brands that want the advertising.

We recognize the damage that social media can cause to how we feel about our physical appearance, but what about how it makes us feel about our wealth or lack thereof?

A symptom of status worry is increased spending and focus on the short term, concluded a report by a new research organization, founded by Martin Lewis, called the Money and Mental Health Policy Institute. It believes that since the financial crisis there has been a steady increase in rates of common mental-health problems, particularly in young people aged between sixteen and twenty-four. While all young people have been affected by a less stable jobs market and insecure housing, which it believes is 'undoubtedly' having a major impact on a generation's mental health, there is equally a heavy pressure to present an idealized image of yourself living your best life. This creates an 'inevitable disparity between the lives [people] feel they are living and those they see portrayed by their friends online. The combination of day-to-day financial insecurity and the idealized world of social media appears to be creating a toxic cocktail.'

The Money and Mental Health Policy Institute was set up in 2016 to research the link between cash and our health, arguing that a lot of good work has been done to support people with mental-health problems who are in problem debt, 'but barely anything has been done to consider how we prevent it happening in the first place'.

Brian Dow, managing director at Mental Health UK, helped set up another charity, the Mental Health and Money Advice Service, in November 2017 because, he says: 'Money problems are widespread and they're causing an awful lot of people stress and worry on a daily basis. That's not healthy. We know that mental health and money problems often go hand in hand. Both are thought of as "taboo" subjects by many, shrouded in shame and secrecy, which is why debt is sadly so often cited as a factor in suicides.'

Money and unhappiness are a vicious circle. Those with serious mental-health conditions may be unable to carry on earning as normal when in the depths of a crisis, or spend money as a symptom of their illness.

Those who are struggling with their finances, or the way that money makes them feel, are more likely to fall prey to mental-health problems as a consequence. Mind, the mental-health charity, says people in unmanageable debt are 33 per cent more likely than the general population to develop depression and anxiety.

• •

Accept it: no one knows what they are doing

As with that email you starred then forgot about, and now it's been so long that the difficulty and awkwardness of replying has increased a hundredfold, so ignoring your finances will just magnify the grief you feel and the charges you pay on your debt.

But no debt problem is insurmountable. You can even come back from bankruptcy within a relatively short period of time. It is possible to completely wipe the slate clean. Start with the money self-care by not beating yourself up about it or writing yourself off as 'terrible with money'. It's normal to feel that you're no good at handling your money. **According to the FCA, the financial services industry regulator, 24 per cent of UK adults have little or no confidence in managing their money, and 46 per cent say their knowledge of financial matters is low.** Being 'terrible with money' is not a personality trait, or a crap tattoo you got when drunk and have now to forever cover with industrial concealer, but a temporary state of things that you can address with a bit of perseverance.

All the same, I used to consider myself as one of those people who are doomed to be terrible with money. I'm useless at maths, my brain fogs over like a bus window on a cold day when I try to interpret graphs or spreadsheets, and I really like buying stuff.

I have since realized that lots of other people, even those who mock me for being scatty, are also in a similar position, big fans of shopping, but not of saving, not very good at understanding their energy bill, or at reading the terms and conditions (no one EVER reads all the terms and conditions) – they just don't admit it. I am continually surprised by how many professional people who read *The Times* write to me in despair, or outrage, that they have been caught out, because they have made what many might consider to be obvious errors, like not realizing that Amazon Prime auto-renews after the free trial period.

Who tells you otherwise until you have made an expensive mistake that you can learn from? The entire, multi-billion-pound credit-card industry works on the basis that humans are fallible, prone to undersaving and overspending, with a phobia for maths and greyed-out text. Amazon had a recorded message on its customer-services line telling you what to do if you had realized you had been paying £79 a year for Prime that you have never used. It knew a lot of people would be calling.

I can now, unbelievably, call myself an enthusiastic runner, despite a couple of years ago being unable to run for longer than thirty seconds without wanting to die. I just decided one day that I was jealous of the people jogging along the canal in the evening sunshine and started Couch to 5k.

Similarly I, and you, can become someone who has a handle on money by just deciding to be so. It is that easy, regardless of how your parents, old flatmates or wealthy accountant sibling remember you at your worst. Write off what you have already spent, do not look back and do not wallow in guilt about it. Clear yourself a Saturday afternoon and sit down with a cup of tea and your laptop to really address your bank account and bills. Your future spending is all that matters.

Practical steps to feel better

Like recording your diet to figure out what gives you a migraine, so keeping a money diary can help you see clearly when it is that you lose motivation to keep control of your finances, or when you might spend more money than normal to make yourself feel better.

Paul Spencer, policy manager at Mind, says you should record your mood and spending habits and see if any patterns emerge. 'It could be that talking to people about money makes you feel really stressed, or you feel very anxious when you know bills are about to leave your account. Recognizing patterns might help you prepare for a stressful time that's coming up.'

Budgeting can hugely help you wrestle some control of where all your money is going, and why, and see clearly what bills you owe and where. File all your paperwork in one place: payslips, bank statements, bills, receipts. Having a clearly labelled folder of all your important bits is as cleansing as a new pencil case.

Set yourself a regular time, maybe once a week or month, to look at your bills and bank balance, so that things do not get out of hand and feel more difficult to tackle. Chapter 4 should be able to help with some apps to make this easier and keep up good habits, such as putting money in 'pots' for rent or bills as soon as your salary is paid. Try to unpick not only the mistakes you are making but why you might be making them, where any fears about money may stem from, and whether those fears are grounded in reality.

In the US there is a Financial Therapy Association, with financial therapists available to help people reach their financial goals 'by thoughtfully addressing financial challenges, while at the same time attending to the emotional, psychological, behavioural and relational hurdles that are intertwined'. This method is yet to reach the UK, but I think it demonstrates that tackling your money worries is much more than just making a spreadsheet.

Do not go overboard with a budget to the point where you feel sick with self-loathing if you do not meet it, or abandon it as soon as it is not working. Some people's worries about money stem from being too obsessional or too organized about saving. Be realistic, and grant yourself some money for positive, indulgent things, too. We earn money to pay the bills, but also in theory to afford to enjoy our existence. Not all the best things in life are free.

Do confide in someone you trust. Tell a friend or family member about your money concerns and how it may be affecting your mental health. You can also let them know warning signs, so that they know how they can help if they notice you acting differently about money. If that's hard you can get some professional advice, without paying. The Money Advice Service and Citizens Advice Bureau offer face-to-face meetings, free, where you can talk through practical things you might be able to do to get a handle on your finances.

What to do when you feel overwhelmed by your debts

It is never too late to tackle debt, and there is a lot of free anonymous help available out there. You are also very much not alone. The debt charity StepChange estimates that there about 3.3 million experiencing 'severe problem debt', but more than 21 million struggling to pay the bills on time. Two-thirds of its clients in 2017 were under forty, one in seven was under twenty-five. **Debt strikes people with all sorts of salaries, too. StepChange told me that it helped more than 20,500 people who earn between £30,000 and £40,000 in 2016, and more than 7,300 people with incomes above £40,000. Average debts for higher earners totalled £40,422.**

If you feel like you are drowning in money you owe, take a pause and look at who you owe it to and whether or not it is what is known as a 'priority debt'. A credit-card debt is not a priority debt, whereas rental arrears, council-tax arrears, or arrears with your energy supplier, are, because if you do not pay you will lose your home or heating, or – in the case of not paying your council tax – risk going to prison.

If you contact any creditors to explain you are in financial difficulty and you are seeking help, they should give you at least thirty days' 'breathing space' before adding interest or chasing debt. You might need to show that you are doing something proactive to sort your debts – for example have gone through StepChange's debt-remedy tool (more below).

Your bank can take money from your current account if you have a debt with it or another bank in the same group (for example Natwest is in the same group as RBS). If you are struggling, especially with the priority debts mentioned above, you might want to make sure that you keep your salary in a different account.

There are debt-management plans (DMP) available, where companies will take over your debts and write to your creditors for you. You make one central payment to the management company a month. This can slow down the pace at which you need to repay your debt. Avoid companies that will sell you these plans, however. They can be expensive. You can set up a DMP free with charity StepChange, or PayPlan.

You can also apply to have some or all of your debts written off, with a Debt Relief Order, an Individual Voluntary Arrangement, or, as a last resort, bankruptcy. All will damage your credit rating and make it difficult for you to borrow again for the following six years, but they will not ruin your life. The stigma attached is not so great that it should damage your health or sense of self-worth.

If you think any of the above may help, or you want some free anonymous advice, StepChange's online debt-remedy tool is the best place to start. It will offer you a personal budget to help you manage your money, and advice tailored to your situation, with an outline of whether a debt-management plan, or any kind of partial insolvency, may be more appropriate. **The charity says that too many sit on their debts before seeking help. Some 50 per cent of its clients waited a year to get advice, yet in just six months a client with a typical range of debts and arrears could face an additional £2,300 debt through interest charges.**

What you can do about debt if you are very ill

Creditors should consider writing off your debt totally if you are very unwell, either mentally or physically, to the point that you will not recover and will never have a way of repaying your debts. You will need to send some medical evidence of your condition.

The problem of overspending and how to deal with it

When Leah, a fellow money journalist, and I used to work in an office, we sat next to each other, going for lunch most days, hammering cheap white wine on a Friday night, doing karaoke at the Christmas party, gossiping about boyfriends and work. In 2014 when I got back from holiday Leah wasn't in. She'd been admitted to hospital after, out of the blue, 'losing her mind', as she puts it. She had suffered a severe manic episode, and was subsequently diagnosed with bipolar disorder.

This changed her financial life. The loss of earnings for the eight months she could not work, coupled with overspending while manic, cost £25,000.

Leah is very switched on about money, had no debt, had saved up a decent amount of cash towards a mortgage deposit. Her illness altered that, making her feel like cash was meaningless, it was just Monopoly notes. She would hand out £20 to *Big Issue* sellers, buy lots of pairs of shoes that were either too big or too small, bags of clothes as gifts for other people.

She wrote a moving piece about how her illness impacted her financial situation:

> As I lost my grip on the life I had built for myself, I had a new sympathy for how quickly things can unravel and how easy it is to fall through the cracks in society.

> During a high, it is common to feel disinhibited, powerful and creative. I felt an overwhelming sense of optimism, like I was destined for success and everything was bound to go my way.

> One of the reasons people often spend so heavily during this phase of the condition is that they have lots of ideas for business ventures that they are convinced will flourish. Spending often relates to this.

Leah, who is now a vocal campaigner about the link between money and mental health, tells me that most people on a bipolar Facebook group that she is part of have similar tales. Overspending is a common symptom of the condition, so much so that doctors use evidence of unusual overspending as a criterion for diagnosing bipolar disorder.

Leah's parents confiscated her cards when she was struggling with the illness. Some people freeze their cards in blocks of ice so that they cannot use them to overspend, but there are starting to be other more convenient options. The Money and Mental Health Policy Institute created a temporary free browser tool called Shopper Stopper, which allowed people who were worried about their spending to set their own 'opening times' for online shops, in order to stop themselves using them when they felt unwell. This was a pilot and is no longer available, though banks are increasingly taking notice and building similar ideas into their operations, so keep an eye out for developments that might help you.

Barclays is launching carer cards that will allow someone else to have access to your bank account but without you sharing your PIN, so that you may hand over all control of your money to someone else at any time when you feel unable to manage it yourself. The bank is also introducing the ability to block certain shops from your card.

The newer app banks such as Monzo allow you to freeze and unfreeze your debit cards for a period. Monzo has also allowed customers to 'self-exclude' from using their card for gambling websites. **Squirrel is a particularly great one for those who want more spending control. It has incorporated a facility that allows you to put your cash savings into a 'money lock-up', where you can only gain access if you physically travel to a preset geographical location – for example 'my sister's house'. It also helps customers stick to a budget by holding your money in a separate account that you have to plan ahead to access.**

While many banks do not advertise that they let you set spending limits or blocks on cards, you may well be able to get them to freeze your cards temporarily, or set a cap on your account, informally. Try calling them to discuss your options if you have a condition that makes it difficult to control your money at certain times. You could also open a basic bank account, which allows you to spend only what is in your account – you cannot go overdrawn – or obtain a prepaid card. See more on these in chapter 4 on budgeting.

If you are worried about your debts and spending as a result of a mental-health condition, write to your bank or creditor with a letter from your healthcare provider detailing your illness. You can download a form from the Money and Mental Health Policy Institute site to help with this. Your bank and creditors should take a view.

Leah told HMRC, for example, that she was struggling to pay her tax bill. They were really reasonable and offered her a period of grace.

PART THREE

Introduction: doing good with money

Congratulations, you have made it this far! You are finally feeling all right about money. Now to look to the future, and not just your own.

As I highlight at the beginning of this book, doing something 'good' with your cash does not always have to involve generating loads more of it, though a new wave of 'responsible investors' show that you can still make money for yourself while keeping the rest of society, and the planet, in mind.

Under 40s are leading the way in shaping how banking and capitalism might look over the next decade and onwards. My final chapter offers you a few ways in which you can make some positive financial decisions to help change things for the better for everyone else, too.

12
Ethical
Finance

Do you support the National Rifle Association (NRA), and the rule of weapons in the USA? I suspect probably not in mind, or on social media, but financially you may well be using your salary (albeit a very tiny part) to prop up the American gun industry.

If you are saving into a pension automatically through your job and have never considered where it is going, you are worryingly likely to be invested in a company that profits from high-school massacres.

My colleague Patrick Hosking, financial editor of *The Times*, recently pointed out, for example, that a British engineering company called Tomkins, which was in the FTSE 100, owned Smith & Wesson, now part of gun maker American Outdoor. American Outdoor made the assault rifle legally sold to the former student who killed seventeen people in the Parkland Florida high-school shooting in February 2018.

Those who are invested in a tracker fund, which many employee pensions are, own shares in whatever companies pop up in whichever index is being tracked. Some of those may be making a lot of money from what you might consider to be immoral or damaging practices. You own a share, you own a tiny bit of a company. How do you feel about owning a tiny bit of a company that produces civilian firearms? What about one that manufactures chemical weapons?

Research carried out in 2018 by Share Action, the charity that campaigns for responsible investment, showed that only three of nine of the UK's biggest auto-enrolment pension providers exclude companies that profit from chemical and biological weapons from the funds they offer employees. The same pension providers are also failing to support companies with decent records on things that we increasingly care more about as a society. Only two, for example, have laid down any policies to encourage responsible tax conduct in the companies they invest in.

Some of the biggest companies most frequently held in UK pension funds also make money from burning fossil fuels, from gambling addiction and pornography.

Luckily, it is becoming easier for those who care about the environmental and social impact of their money to find places to save and invest to equal advantage. You just need to be aware of it and act. Ethical investment has been around for a long time, with certain funds 'screening out' what are known traditionally as 'sin stocks' – shares in companies that produce, for example, tobacco or alcohol, weapons or gambling products.

More of these are appearing. Following the Parkland shooting, BlackRock, the world's largest asset manager, said that it would exclude gun makers and gun retailers from its socially responsible funds. These already exclude companies that make cluster bombs and cigarettes. BlackRock 'institutional investors' (big investors such as banks and pension providers) can now include gun-free index funds in pension plans available to employees.

In recent years ethical investment has taken a more proactive approach, with what is known as 'impact investing' or 'responsible investing' becoming more common and popular, particularly with a younger, more socially conscious generation. This happens where funds do not just screen out companies, but also choose to invest in companies that meet certain positive 'ESG' (environmental, social and governance) criteria.

Such funds might avoid any oil companies, focusing instead on green energy producers, as well as companies or organizations that improve healthcare and education, or expand board diversity.

In May 2018 the 'Girl fund' was introduced by Dame Helena Morrissey, head of personal investing at Legal & General Investment Management (a total real-life superwoman who also has nine children), as the UK's first fund to consider gender. The fund's official name is the L&G Future World Gender in Leadership UK index fund, and it will allocate more investors' money to those companies that have better gender diversity in their senior ranks weighted by how big a business they are.

• •

Choosing a greener energy supplier

If climate change is a concern, the quickest and easiest way to do something more environmentally considerate with your cash is to switch your energy company to one that uses alternative sources. This used to mean paying loads more, but now most green tariffs are competitively priced and are generally cheaper than hanging around on the standard variable rate of one of the Big Six energy suppliers (EDF, British Gas, SSE, ScottishPower, E.ON and Npower).

Green tariffs either use your money to contribute towards environmental projects, or will match your energy use with generation from alternative sources. The best do a bit of both, as well as being generally smaller, friendlier local organizations with UK-based customer-service teams.

If your energy comes from the national grid, which is the case if you do not generate it at home yourself, then you get electricity from the same place as everyone else whatever supplier you choose. If you go green then your green supplier will add back into the system the amount that you have used in renewable energy.

Companies such as Good Energy and Ecotricity add back 100 per cent. Good Energy's electricity is sourced from solar, wind, hydro and biofuel. It also offers 'green gas', 6 per cent of which comes from biomethane, which is produced in the UK from our waste, such as sewage. The rest is

made carbon-neutral through carbon-reduction schemes.

There is controversy over how much of an impact green tariffs make, because of the 'Renewable Energy Guarantee of Origin' scheme (REGO). Government rules that every unit of electricity created from a renewable source gets a REGO certificate. Green suppliers produce a lot of these, but they are bought and sold too, and other less green suppliers buy them up to create their own claim to be 100 per cent renewable based purely on having paid for some certificates.

Because there is a market for them, green suppliers are effectively subsidizing non-green ones. It is complicated, and if you have concerns I'd recommend reading up on how it all works.

Nevertheless if you sign up with a genuinely green company, such as the ones mentioned above (also check out Octopus and Bulb), your money is helping to push the agenda. Octopus invests in solar generation, building solar farms; Good Energy supports the UK's small energy generators.

Choosing a more responsible bank

While it looks like the money in your current or savings account just sits there, waiting for you to withdraw it, the 'deposits' you make are in fact used by banks to invest elsewhere, to make loans to businesses or to buy complex financial 'instruments' overseas.

If you want more control over where and to whom your money is being loaned, consider an ethical bank. Two of the most transparent are Charity Bank and Triodos.

Charity Bank offers a range of fixed and easy-access savings accounts with competitive rates of interest that use your savings to make loans to charities and social enterprises providing everything from affordable housing to football training for people with disabilities.

Triodos is a Dutch bank but with a UK office, that lends money only to people and organizations within the UK that it believes will deliver 'real social, cultural or environmental

benefits', such as organic farms, therapy centres and youth projects. Triodos also has savings accounts, including cash ISAs, easy-access savers and fixed-rate bonds, investment funds and a current account, which has a £3 a month usage fee.

Both banks pride themselves on being up front, so that you can see exactly how your money is being used and the variety of organizations they lend to is outlined in full on their websites.

• •

Choosing an environmentally friendly mortgage

If you are in the market to buy a place, you might want to consider a new 'green mortgage'. In 2018 Barclays introduced a discount on its up to 90 per cent LTV mortgages, including Help to Buy loans, for those who buy a newbuild energy-efficient property with an energy-performance certificate rating of A or B built by one of a select few developers.

Ecology Building Society lends specifically to those renovating or converting a property with sustainability and energy efficiency in mind, or building a sustainable property from scratch. Building societies in general are a better bet for corporate ethos. They are smaller and more local than the UK's biggest banks, and often have competitive rates and kinder terms. Nationwide is the biggest, but smaller building societies such as Newbury, Leek United and Yorkshire Building Society appear in best-buy tables for rates.

• •

Responsible pensions and investments

If you have been automatically enrolled into your company pension you are probably in its default fund. These often have low fees, which means they are more likely to be tracker funds rather than 'actively managed' (more on what this means in chapter 6). The index that a tracker follows will be made up of all sorts of profitable companies, many of which might be funding industries that do not align with your principles. You can move out of the default fund easily, and many workplace pension schemes will offer an ethical fund that you can invest in if you know to ask.

Scrutinize where exactly the ethical fund is invested, though, and whether it invests for positive impact or simply screens out companies that it decides are 'unethical'. Some may contain oil companies, for example, on the basis that an oil company may have set up a solar project, even if 90 per cent of its profits still come from fossil fuels. Or, as pointed out by Jeannie Boyle, director at financial advice firm EQ Investors, you could end up with a weapons manufacturer that scores highly for the treatment of its staff.

If you are self-employed you have more choice. The National Employment Savings Trust (NEST) is the only major auto-enrolment pension provider that Share Action found had a target to reduce its portfolio's exposure to climate-related financial risks, and its ethical fund invests in companies with positive records on fair trade policies, the environment, human rights and fair labour practices and is also a good place to start an independent pension.

There is a growing number of ethical investment funds available to include in a self-invested personal pension, or as part of an investment portfolio or investment ISA, too.

The advisers 3D Investing specialize in ethical investments and suggest a list of 201 funds that focus on positive ESG goals. EQ Investors, the wealth manager, has a series of 'positive impact portfolios', made up of twenty to twenty-five diversified funds each. Since 2017 it has been using the United Nations' Sustainable Development Goals to think about impact, using the goals as a framework to make fund selections. Holdings range from a company that aims to give ex-prisoners living-wage jobs in the construction industry in Glasgow, to a Norwegian company that offers an alternative to overfishing, and a Japanese innovator that manufactures composite materials from carbon fibre.

The objection to 'ethical investing' that has always been raised is that being green or 'worthy' is costly. If you have been reading this book you are probably saving and investing in order to have more money. Well – result – doing so ethically no longer means sacrificing a decent return. In fact, people are starting to believe exactly the opposite.

EQ Investors' annual impact report showed evidence that investing in companies making a positive impact should be good for returns. Guns and fossil fuels are no longer looking such a safe bet, as governments around the world legislate against them and citizens start to question whether they should exist. Whether you look at revenues or profits, the companies held by the EQ Positive Impact Portfolios are growing significantly faster than the FTSE 100 companies, its report found.

When Rebecca O'Connor founded the website Good with Money, which has useful guides and recommendations on making ethical choices with your personal finances, it was annoyance that drove her.

She writes: 'I was annoyed that I'd heard a respected City veteran proudly state that there was no place for ethics in investment decisions to a nodding room of suits, when such a shameless expression of immorality and greed would provoke horror in any other context.'

She says, however, that the idea that taking an ethical view on your money means compromise on financial return is outdated. 'There is study after study from some really large, well respected investment banks, that show that the financial performance has actually been better for funds that have an ESG theme over the long term.'

It makes sense: the companies offering the solutions we need may make more profit over time than those companies exacerbating the problems, especially as socially conscious young people are set to inherit the baby boomers' invested wealth.

So I will end here on one of the greatest positives that have sprung from the financial crisis a decade on: a sense that we might be able to put some pressure on those responsible by voting with our debit cards. Money and knowledge are power, even if you only have a small amount of each. Collectively it adds up, and the younger generation are already starting to convince the suits that their old model needs a tweak.

Research from Schroders, the asset manager, found that 52 per cent of millennials prefer to invest with sustainability in mind – a far higher proportion than their parents.

By now you should feel a bit more confident about your own money situation, which means you can at least start to think about whether you could do something better with your savings, whatever you decide that should be.

We all have a choice about how we think about money, what we do with money, where and how we save it, and how we let it make us and those around us feel. Spend forth and use it well.

THANKS

I shall be forever grateful to Ruth Lewy for introducing me to the amazing Michelle Kane at 4th Estate, who imagined this book and invited me into the 4th Estate family. It has been a total pleasure to work with you Michelle, Naomi Mantin, Tara Al Azzawi and team. Thanks for your vision, enthusiasm and encouragement, and to Jack Smyth for making a book about personal finance look so beautiful.

This book is a compilation of answers to all the questions and dilemmas shared with me by my brilliant friends, friends of friends and assorted fellow millennials, as well as *Times* readers. Thanks to you all for being honest about money, and what you do not know, for your emails, phone calls, tweets and long pub conversations pondering the state we are in, in particular Lauren and Rose Manister and Matt Davies, who have tolerated a disproportionate number, and Guy Bolton and Franca Bernatavicius for your advice. I am especially indebted to those who write in to *The*

Times Troubleshooter every week to challenge the arrogance of big companies, and to advertise their misfortunes so that others may be spared.

Of course I could not have compiled the answers without the help of real, qualified financial experts, campaigning organizations, researchers and fellow consumer journalists too many to list here, but whom I have cited throughout. Thanks for so generously sharing with me what you know. Special mention to my super smart colleagues Leah Milner, Mark Bridge, and Mark Atherton for reading chapters and making exceptional cups of tea, to my present *Times* editors, Anne Ashworth and Carol Lewis, for your support, and to my old bosses Andrew Ellson and David Budworth for taking a punt on a clueless 23-year-old. Sorry my French is not as good as my CV led you to believe.

Bengt, I would struggle to achieve anything without your never-ending supply of love, patience, original ideas and aubergine pasta, least of all manage to write a book. Thanks for never judging my spending habits. And, to the rest of the team: Ruth, Mum and Dad, who taught me that you should acknowledge the power of money, but never let it rule and who loaned me quite a lot of it.